AT HOME

AT HOME

An Illustrated
History of Houses and Homes

By
Anthony Ridley

CRANE RUSSAK : NEW YORK

Published in the United States in 1976 by
Crane, Russak & Co Inc
347 Madison Avenue, New York NY 10017
ISBN 0–8448–0916–0
Library of Congress Catalogue Card Number 75–43446

Printed in Great Britain

Contents

I

The Development of the House

The house is man's age-old response to the need for shelter. It has taken many forms according to the material resources of its builders and the problems set them by their environment. Today's glass and concrete apartment blocks, designed for urban living, are the direct descendants of the mud huts of the earliest agricultural villages.

Mankind was born half a million or more years ago into the sun-kissed continent of Africa, where life could be lived out-of-doors all year round with little hardship. Perhaps the first home was nothing more than a heap of brushwood arranged as a windbreak around an otherwise open camp. Eventually, however, men pushed their way into less hospitable regions under whose wintry skies survival without adequate shelter was impossible.

Faced with the necessity of finding a refuge from the elements, our ancestors seem to have sought out natural caverns. Such sites were few and far between but, in those days, so were people. The earliest signs of human activity to the north of the frost line come from the Choukoutien caves near Peking in China, which have yielded many skeletal fragments of primitive men. But bones were not the only finds. Traces of fires lit 360,000 years ago have also been unearthed. The ancient inhabitants of China had learnt to value their creature comforts, and the caves which they cheered with their fire-light must be amongst the oldest dwelling places that will ever be discovered.

As the human population of the colder lands gradually increased, ready-made homes inevitably became more difficult to find. Men were driven out into the open where they learnt to build effective shelters of their own. The earliest man-made dwellings for which evidence has so far been found were built by the mammoth hunters who inhabited southern Russia over 20,000 years ago. Climatic conditions were still very severe in the declining stages of the last Ice Age, but the hunters and their families contrived to hold the cold at bay by scooping out shelters in the ground. Some of these crude pit houses have been thoroughly excavated. Low walls of

7

mammoths' skulls and long bones were built around a sunken floor area, and a tent-like roof of animal pelts was raised on a framework of tusks and branches. The wind was kept out by weighting down the skirts of the skin covering with mammoths' shoulder blades.

Huts with dug-out floors gave reasonable head-room for a minimum height of wall. They were also virtually draught proof. This style of building continued in many areas through countless generations. It survived the extinction of the mammoth and adapted itself to new materials, so that earth, stone, timber, and thatch replaced the original bone and skin. It outlasted dramatic changes in culture, sheltering some of the earliest men to give up the wandering life of the hunter and herdsmen for the settled existence of the farmer. Pit dwellings were, in fact, known down to medieval times and were common in Saxon England.

Reconstruction of the dwellings built by mammoth hunters in eastern Europe over 20,000 years ago.

Between ten and twelve thousand years ago the world was beginning to thaw out as the last Ice Age came to an end. As the glaciers retreated from Europe and North America, warmer, wetter conditions spread across the world. Rainfall in the Middle East, the homeland of such cereals as wheat and barley, was far more copious than today, and much of what is now desert was fertile. The time was ripe for people to take the vital step from collecting wild edible grasses to planting and tending crops of their own. Farming villages began to spring up throughout the hill country of the Middle East. This change to a settled life of tilling the fields encouraged the development of substantial houses meant to last a life-time.

One of the earliest agricultural settlements yet discovered is at Jericho, which lies beside an oasis in modern Jordan. This well-watered site was first used as a seasonal camping ground by nomadic hunters at least as early as the ninth millennium B.C., but by about 7000 B.C. occupation had become permanent and the way of life had changed to farming. The dwellings of the 2,000 inhabitants were clay brick or wattle-and-daub, curved-walled huts with sunken floors. The village was protected by a dry-stone rampart 6 feet (1·8 m.) high, but, despite this impressive line of defence, it seems to have been conquered by outsiders with different traditions. Archaeologists have detected a sudden alteration in the cultural

Reconstruction of the strange, interlocking houses of Çatal Hüyük.

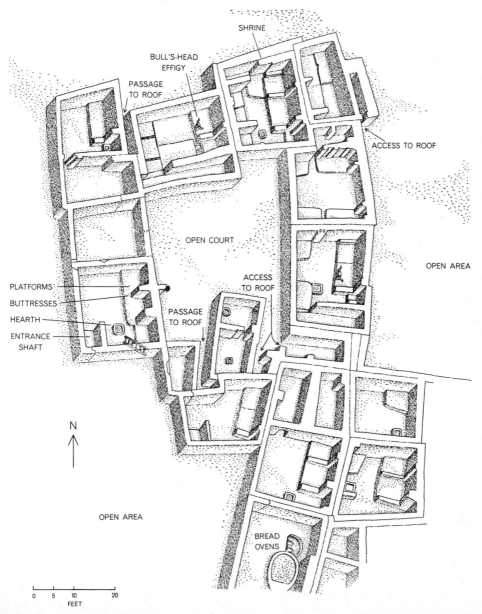

SHRINE

BULL'S-HEAD
EFFIGY

PASSAGE
TO ROOF

ACCESS TO ROOF

OPEN COURT

OPEN AREA

PLATFORMS

BUTTRESSES

ACCESS
TO ROOF

HEARTH

PASSAGE
TO ROOF

ENTRANCE
SHAFT

N
↑

OPEN AREA

BREAD
OVENS

0   5   10   20
FEET

pattern of the settlement from about 6800 B.C., when the simple round huts gave place to large rectangular houses, each with several rooms. A new style of mud-brick construction was used, and frequently the rooms were grouped around a courtyard. The type of dwelling that is still typical of the Middle East had appeared.

Rectangular houses were not peculiar to Jericho alone. They occur at Jarmo, a village of comparable antiquity discovered in Iraq, and have also been found at the interesting Turkish site of Çatal Hüyük. This was virtually a city, although it is thought to date back as far as the seventh millennium B.C. It was, however, a strange town without streets or normal doors. The mud-brick houses were built one against the other, without even the narrowest lane between; the only open spaces were inner courtyards. Outer walls were blank and featureless—giving protection against flood water and enemy attack. All access to individual houses was by way of the roofs, and each front door was merely a hole in the ceiling.

Like agriculture, the rectilinear style of building spread into Europe, but it was by no means universally accepted. Other traditions were at work, and even where rectangular houses came into prominence the altered climatic conditions often dictated changes in both design and materials. The mud-brick eastern dwelling, looking inwards to a shaded courtyard, was ideal for a hot, sunny country with only moderate rainfall. In wetter climates mud brick was not a suitable building material, nor was it necessary to shut out the sun. Northern Greece in the sixth millennium B.C. was dry enough for mud brick to be used, but its houses were free-standing, single-roomed structures, each separated from its neighbours. In European villages the houses characteristically stood apart rather than clustered together Asian fashion. This was as true in eastern and central Europe, where the rectangular house plan was generally adopted, as in the west which for long retained its native circular huts.

Round houses remained the predominant form of dwelling along the Atlantic coast of Europe and in Britain until well into Roman times. Strabo, a Greek geographer of the first century B.C., described the Celtic houses of his time as large, circular structures built of timber and wicker-work and roofed with thatch. It was a kind of shelter well adapted to the needs of a damp climate and the natural resources of a well-wooded region.

East of the river Rhine in the stronghold of the rectangular house, the choice of building material was again influenced by local availability. In the heavily forested areas timber was used to provide a framework, and mud was employed merely for plastering. Elsewhere the less substantial wattle-and-daub, a means of building in which walls were formed by weaving thin twigs between a series of poles prior to plastering with mud, was common. But whatever the mode of building, the oriental flat roof was usually replaced by a gabled structure with a central ridge.

The wattle-and-daub houses of fourth millennium B.C. Bulgaria were often of the megaron type which seems to have originated in western Asia. This form of house, with a porch in front of the main room, was widely adopted in the Balkans, and much later became the prototype for the classical Greek temple. Surviving pottery models of Bulgarian megarons show them to have had gabled roofs and round window openings. Markings on the models suggest that exteriors were decorated with swirling designs,

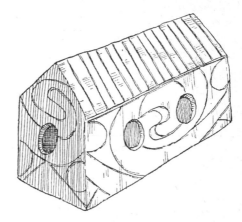

An example of the fourth millennium B.C. house models found on Bulgarian sites which show the adoption of the gabled roof, well-suited to a wet climate.

while archaeological evidence indicates that interior walls were plastered and painted with horizontal stripes of white and maroon.

The Bulgarian farmers favoured small, single-family dwellings, but their contemporaries in Rumania and a large belt of country stretching west as far as modern Brussels preferred community living. They built huge rectangular houses often 100 feet (30 m.) long and 25 feet (7·6 m.) wide. Within these massive timber-framed structures lived several families sheltered by a gabled roof, which was supported by up to three rows of vertical posts.

While the barbarians of Europe still inhabited their long houses, the first civilizations of the world were emerging in the Middle East. Farmers along the Tigris, Euphrates, and the Nile had learnt the art of irrigation agriculture, and were able to produce food in excess of their immediate needs. Specialized craftsmen were freed from the necessity of labour on the land. Instead they could concentrate on their skills and exchange their goods for the products of the farmers' fields. Rulers and priestly castes appeared to batten on the efforts of the peasants. Society became complex, and cities grew up.

By about 3000 B.C. Mesopotamia and Egypt each possessed many populous cities with mud-brick houses crowded along narrow, tortuous alleys. Both cultures favoured the cool courtyard dwelling, but the Egyptians never developed this type of building to the same extent as the Sumerians of Mesopotamia. Existing Egyptian models show houses built along only two sides of the yard, which was enclosed on its other flanks by plain walls. But this was not the only kind of Egyptian home. Other models show compact block houses, while paintings reveal that at a later date multi-storey dwellings had become common in some congested cities. A four-storey house is clearly shown in a mural from Thebes, the Egyptian capital from 1580 to 1085 B.C.

A house model made in ancient Egyptian times.

The Mesopotamian town house is perhaps best represented by the early second millennium B.C. homes excavated at the Sumerian city of Ur. Probably these dwellings belonged to prosperous families, but they are still impressive for their size and comfort. Each stood two-storeys high and contained thirteen or fourteen rooms, all of which faced inwards to a totally enclosed courtyard. Blank outer walls, broken only by an entrance door and a few ventilation grills, threw back the glare of the sun and kept out the noise of the street. An inner staircase led up to a wooden balcony that jutted out over the courtyard and gave access to the upper rooms.

By now, when the Sumerian and Egyptian civilizations were already a thousand years old, other peoples were founding cities. The town houses of Sumeria were matched by those of Minoan Crete and the Indus Valley. Along the Indus, where the climate was not unlike that of Mesopotamia,

Egyptian four-storey house from a Theban wall-painting.

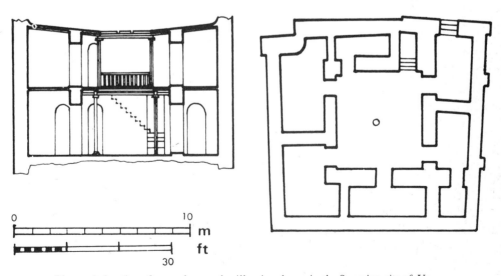

Plan and elevation of an early second millennium house in the Sumerian city of Ur.

the courtyard plan predominated, and dwellings developed that were very similar to those at Ur. Mohenjo-daro for instance, an Indus city which flourished from about 2300 to 1750 B.C., contained many two-storey, courtyard houses boasting such luxuries as bathrooms and water-flushed lavatories. In the poorer quarters of this city, however, monotonous rows of much simpler homes, each consisting of only two rooms flanking a diminutive yard, have been discovered.

Island Crete, with its sea-tempered climate, produced a different style of architecture. The palaces of the Minoan civilization of the second millennium B.C. were built around courts and light-wells, but private houses were well supplied with outward-looking windows. A fortunate survival provides a fascinating glimpse of a whole range of Minoan homes. Many fragments have been recovered from what was perhaps once an inlay meant to depict a town. On assembly, the various pieces revealed a number of separate porcelain plaques, each showing the façade of an individual dwelling. From these it can be seen that Minoan houses rose to two or sometimes three storeys, and that although the upper floors had many windows the door was generally the only opening at street level. Perhaps the Minoans lived upstairs over ground-floor store-rooms.

Minoan civilization reached the peak of its power in the sixteenth century B.C., when its fleet dominated Mediterranean trade. Cretan merchants ranged widely, carrying their island's produce to Egypt, Phoenicia, Greece, and Italy. But great travellers though the Minoans were, their world was bounded by the Mediterranean. They went about their business unaware of the rise in distant China of a culture which was to outlast their own by 3,000 years and survive down to modern times.

Historical China dates from about 1600 B.C., when the semi-legendary warlord, Tang, established the Shang Dynasty by winning ascendancy

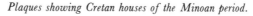

Plaques showing Cretan houses of the Minoan period.

Pottery model of a rich man's house from Han dynasty China.

over the many local chieftains of the Yellow River region. Even before this time Chinese society had reached a fairly sophisticated level. Sizable towns, needing the support of a highly advanced agriculture, already existed early in the second millennium B.C. A settlement unearthed at Ch'eng-tzu-yai occupied a rectangular area 1,500 by 1,300 feet (460 × 400 m.), completely enclosed by a defensive wall. The houses of this period were, however, still comparatively primitive, the circular hut with sunken floor being greatly favoured. Under the Shang a rectangular form of building began to predominate, but even in the huge capital city of Anyang, founded in 1384 B.C., only the simplest constructional materials were used. Palace and hovel alike were built from mud, timber, and thatch.

Dynasties prospered and declined. Shang was supplanted by Chou; Chou by Chin; Chin by Han. But through it all the continuity of Chinese culture remained unbroken. By Han times, about 200 B.C. to about A.D. 200, China had grown into a populous country with about fifty million inhabitants, many of whom lived in towns. Architecture had also advanced, and although the poorer people still sheltered beneath the thatch of flimsy wattle huts, the rich by now lived in multi-storey, timber-framed homes. 15

An examination of the numerous clay model houses recovered from Han graves reveals no one uniform type. Some models show houses climbing in a series of diminishing steps to three or four storeys, each storey having its own wide-eaved, tiled roof. Others depict humbler dwellings with sometimes only one storey ranged along two sides of an enclosed court. It is a tribute to the tenacity of this most long-lasting of civilizations that the single-storey courtyard house remains the traditional Chinese dwelling to the present day.

While China went on always somehow keeping its culture alive despite civil war and foreign invasion, Europe witnessed the rise and fall of Greece and Rome, the two classical civilizations that contributed most to the Western heritage. The Greeks were an amazingly talented people. Even in the early eighth century B.C., when they had hardly emerged from a dark age of warfare and chaos, they could produce the literary genius of Homer. By the fifth century B.C., the golden age of Greece, their abilities had reached full maturity. Science and mathematics soared to new heights; drama was born; sculptors and architects achieved miracles of beauty. The official buildings of the Greek cities of this period have perhaps never been bettered, but this splendour was not passed down to the ordinary house. Greek interest was concentrated on public life rather than domestic ostentation.

Two distinct traditions seem to have influenced the design of Greek houses. The free-standing megaron, with its porch and gabled roof, came into Greece from the colder lands to the north; the courtyard dwelling was introduced from the east. House models of eighth century B.C. origin unearthed near Corinth were of the megaron type, with columns supporting a roof which jutted out at the front to form a porch. Within two hundred years, however, the courtyard house had become well established. The sixth-century homes excavated on the off-shore island of Aegina each consisted of two or three rooms grouped around a small walled enclosure. From at least this time the inward-looking house predominated in Greek towns, but sometimes the rival styles of building were married by turning the principal room into a megaron which opened on to the courtyard through a colonnaded porch.

The fifth-century dwellings that lined the straight streets of Olynthus, a planned city in Chalcidice to the north of the Aegean Sea, made no such concession to the megaron tradition. Excavation has shown them to be of the so-called pastas type, taking their name from the narrow principal room that presented its long side to the courtyard. The pastas normally lay to the north of the court, which was flanked by other rooms to the east and west and separated from the street by a wall along its south side. Stairs led up from the courtyard to an upper storey. Houses sometimes contained eight rooms on the ground floor alone, so accommodation could hardly be called cramped. On the other hand building methods were somewhat primitive. The floors at ground level were frequently mere beaten earth, while walls were made of unbaked bricks. Roofs, however, were probably tiled. Many houses possessed bathrooms, but sanitation was completely lacking.

Three hundred years later the houses of the Greek island of Delos, although retaining the same basic courtyard plan, showed great structural improvement. Now the floors were for the most part of carefully laid mosaic, the walls were of stone, and, luxury of luxuries, each house possessed its own lavatory emptying into an underground drain. Peristyle courts, enclosed on all sides by elegant colonnades, gave dwellings an added dignity. However, not all the families of Delos could afford a whole house to themselves. External stairways leading to the upper storeys of some Delian buildings strongly suggest the existence of flats.

Many of the ordinary people of the great city of Rome, whose power overshadowed the Greek world from about 200 B.C., were also flat-dwellers. Multi-storey buildings were adopted as a solution to the problem of cramming a rising population into a comparatively small area. In an age before public transport towns were necessarily compact. Citizens needed to be within walking distance of the centre, and even at the height of its prosperity, in the second century A.D., Rome's area was never allowed to exceed eight square miles. By this time five-storey blocks of flats were commonplace, while what few single-family houses existed were owned by the very wealthy. A survey made early in the fourth century revealed that Rome contained over 46,000 tenement buildings, the so-called 'insulae', but only about 1,800 private homes.

From a distance Rome's tall, window-studded insulae had a surprisingly modern appearance. It was only on closer inspection that the deficiencies became apparent. Some short-comings were fundamental. Especially in the earlier days, construction was so flimsy that the collapse of whole blocks was alarmingly frequent. In an effort to avert further tragedies the Emperor Augustus, who ruled at the beginning of the Christian era, set a 65-foot (20-m.) limit on the height of new buildings. But this did little to improve the standard of workmanship, and a century later the satirist, Juvenal, could still mock at a Rome where towering flats were held up by nothing more substantial than 'beams as long and thin as flutes'.

Not only did life in a Roman insula involve very real dangers, it also had a number of petty irritations and discomforts. The windows, for all they

Model of Roman flats at Ostia. The modern-looking exterior hides many deficiencies.

looked so grand from the outside, were completely devoid of glass. Window panes, though known, were too expensive for ordinary pockets, and tenement dwellers often had to choose between a roaring gale blowing round their ears and a room prematurely darkened by the closure of wooden shutters. In winter things got particularly miserable, since the lack of either fireplace or hypocaust heating forced the inhabitants of the insulae to rely on pitifully feeble charcoal braziers. On a cold night the rule was very much: 'Early to bed'.

A deficiency, which must have been felt the whole year round, was the complete lack of plumbing. Aqueducts poured millions of gallons of water into Rome every day, but none found its way directly into the insulae. Only the wealthy occupants of private houses had water on tap; ordinary people fetched theirs from streets fountains, and then faced the wearying task of carrying it upstairs. No wonder the Romans flocked in such numbers to the public baths. It could have been no fun washing at home.

Tenement dwellers were little better served in the matter of sanitation. They had to share a communal privy built over a rarely emptied cesspool on the ground floor, and rather than brave this smelly hole, many must have gone out during the day to the far more salubrious public lavatories, which discharged into proper sewers. At night-time it was a common, though illegal, practice for upper-floor tenants to empty the contents of their chamber pots out of the windows. The late-night reveller had to beware the rattle of an opening shutter.

In sharp contrast to the towering insulae, the home of a well-to-do Roman seldom exceeded two storeys, with the upper floor, even then, usually given over to slave accommodation. Below lay the principal apartments, set out in a formal pattern owing much to Etruscan influence. The central hall, or atrium, lit by a small roof-opening, was in the best Etruscan tradition; so was the symmetrical arrangement of the surrounding apartments. In a typical house a hallway flanked by several minor rooms gave access to the atrium with its central rainwater tank set beneath the skylight. Beyond lay the main family room, which opened on to an enclosed garden. The richness of the décor and the number and size of the subsidiary chambers on either side of the atrium were dictated by the wealth of the owner. As so far described the form was purely Italian, but from the second century B.C. onwards Greek example made it increasingly fashionable to extend the garden into a peristyle court with additional rooms grouped around it.

The Romans carried their architectural ideas into conquered regions. A few important cities, most notably Constantinople, the capital of the empire from A.D. 330, even built tall blocks of flats after the style of the Roman insulae, but it was the inward-looking private house or domus, which was most widely copied. In Britain alone over 500 villas have so far been discovered, the grander ones built around courtyards in the Italian manner. Some concessions were, however, made to the cooler northern climate. Important rooms were heated by hot air passed through floor and wall ducts, while the colonnade of the peristyle court, which even in sunny Italy was sometimes enclosed, was usually replaced by a windowed corridor. The unroofed atrium proved particularly unsuited to British conditions and is seldom found.

For the first four centuries of the Christian era Rome dominated the Mediterranean world and much of western Europe. Throughout all this wide territory the rich aped Roman custom, but the veneer of civilization was often very thin. In the distant province of Britain the life of the ordinary people was little affected by the Roman presence. Their native villages still consisted of rude one-roomed huts. Little wonder then that in such a region the Roman tradition of domestic building did not long outlast the disastrous collapse of the Western Empire under the pressure of successive barbarian invasions during the fifth century. Villas crumbled into ruins and were forgotten, and fourteen hundred years had to pass before western Europe again produced houses of comparable comfort.

The Anglo-Saxon invaders who overran the abandoned Roman province of Britain during the fifth and sixth centuries brought their own primitive style of building with them from the Continent. Archaeological evidence suggests that most of these settlers lived in small huts with sunken floors. Noblemen, however, maintained long houses or halls within which their followers led communal lives, eating at the same table and sleeping on the same earthen floor. Wood was the basic structural material of these buildings, which, because of their considerable length, must have possessed a certain simple dignity. The walls consisted of closely spaced timber uprights made weather-tight by a cladding of wattle-and-daub or planks. Even the gabled roofs may sometimes have consisted of wooden shingles, though at an earlier date thatch was probably almost universally used. Some halls were wide enough for their roofs to require the support of one or more rows of wooden posts, running the length of the building. Occasionally these columns were placed directly under the crest of the roof along the axis of the house, but a much more common arrangement was the double row, which gave the hall two side aisles.

The Bayeux Tapestry, which was made shortly after the Norman conquest of England, gives a glimpse of housing conditions in northern Europe in the second half of the eleventh century. Amongst its many scenes the tapestry shows a nobleman's hall and several peasant cottages. King Harold's hall at Bosham is depicted as a long room, built over a vaulted ground-floor cellar, and approached by an easily defended external stairway. This type of first-floor dwelling, which combined the advantages of added security with plentiful storage space, retained its popularity for several

King Harold's hall from the Bayeux Tapestry.

The first-floor living quarters in the twelfth-century manor-house at Boothby Pagnell were approached by an external staircase.

centuries. The cottages too, though extremely humble, would not have seemed out of place in many parts of Europe two hundred years later. They were single-roomed and windowless, and, since their roofs were unbroken by any hole, seem even to have lacked the elementary comfort of an internal fireplace. About the most that could be said for them was that they were weatherproof. Of the three cottages shown, one gives the impression of being built from stone blocks, the others from overlapping wooden planks. All three were probably roofed with wooden shingles.

Gradually the quality of European life improved. The wooden hall, so dear to the Saxon aristocrat's heart, became a thing of the past, and the nobility habitually built in stone. By the thirteenth century some French countrymen were building themselves two-roomed stone houses provided with fireplaces for heating and cooking, while in towns such as Cluny the dwellings of wealthy merchants had for long soared to three storeys. England, in general, lagged behind these standards. A late thirteenth-century survey compiled for taxation purposes on the houses around Colchester in Essex revealed that only one in ten had more than a single room.

But lowland England was potentially a rich country, and as the Middle Ages waned wealth became a little more evenly spread. Many people were lifted from subsistence level to a position where they could afford better accommodation. The two-roomed farmhouse with a hall, or communal living-room, and a separate sleeping chamber for the master became increasingly common. Sometimes a third room was added over the chamber, 21 but throughout the English medieval period the hall, great or small, extended up to the roof. The beautiful carpentry of the beams was used as a decorative feature.

The pressure on space inside tightly walled cities led English townsmen to pile one storey on another long before their country cousins. Lincoln still boasts a pair of two-storey houses whose solid stone-work has survived from the twelfth century, while the early prevalence of storeyed dwellings in London is proved by a building ordinance of 1189 which enjoined citizens to build fire-proof party walls to the surprising height of 16 feet (4·9 m.). Accommodation was, however, very simple; probably nothing more than one room to each floor, with a ladder to connect them.

It was only in later centuries that permanent staircases were installed in any but the best homes, or that additional rooms were considered desirable. During the Middle Ages the usual urban building plot was long and narrow, so to make the most of its site a house had to extend backwards from the street to which it presented its gabled end. This was the origin of the tall, deep building so typical of the late medieval city. Upper storeys were allowed to project, giving further living-space. By the end of the fifteenth century three-storey timber-framed houses were common in many English towns.

Tradition and a continuing abundance of timber ensured that building in wood retained its popularity over much of England, Germany, and Scandinavia long after less heavily forested countries had begun to adopt alternative materials. The art of brick-making, which had almost been lost

A twelfth-century house in the city of Lincoln.

The sixteenth-century front of Staple Inn in London gives a good idea of the appearance of town houses of the period.

on the fall of the Roman Empire, was re-learnt by the people of the Lowlands during the twelfth century. Brick houses had been an accepted norm in the trim towns of the Netherlands for two hundred years, when a sixteenth-century Spanish visitor to London wrote in disgust that the English built their homes of 'sticks and dirt'. The Scottish King James VI, who ascended the English throne in 1603, was equally appalled by the condition of his new capital. With the vision of stone-built Edinburgh fresh in his mind he rashly declared that he would transform the city 'from stykkes to brykkes'. But it took more than the brave words of a king to persuade Londoners to abandon their jettied, timber-framed skyscrapers, whose protruding upper storeys turned the narrow lanes into virtual tunnels. It was only after the Great Fire of 1666 had claimed 13,000 houses that a substantial rebuilding in brick took place.

Brick was only one aspect of progress; the changing climate of European taste was at last having an effect on the conservative English middle classes. The ideal of symmetry, pioneered by the architects of Renaissance Italy, achieved wider acceptance, and buildings took on a fresh dignity. Speculative builders like Nicholas Barbon began to extend London's northern boundary 23

Late seventeenth-century houses in Gray's Inn Square, London.

with large-scale suburban developments. Barbon's Red Lion Square, which was commenced in 1684, consisted of terraces of tall, brick houses, very much after the Italian fashion. For the first time Englishmen were induced to live in streets where each house was a replica of its neighbours. This innovation was to lead both to the restrained elegance of the Georgian crescent and the dreary monotony of the Victorian industrial town.

The European settlers who poured into North America in increasing numbers during the seventeenth century carried a variety of building traditions with them to their new country. At first they were too busy carving a living out of the wilderness to erect more than make-shift shelters, but once the land was tamed their thoughts turned to permanent homes. The houses they built, though modelled on familiar European patterns, were adapted to the requirements of the new environment. Along the heavily forested northern Atlantic seaboard, where English influence was strong, wood was the usual building material. The timber framing of most houses was typical of the mother country, but the covering that converted gaunt wooden skeletons into weatherproof homes was different. Instead of an infilling of bricks or plaster to close the gaps between the ribs, a cladding of clapboard was attached to the beams. Concessions were also made to the severe winter climate. Windows were kept fairly small to reduce heat losses, while a type of house became popular in which rooms clustered for warmth around a central chimney.

But the English tradition was not the only one at work. The early seventeenth-century Swedish colony on the Delaware introduced the type of house whose image was to be enshrined in American folklore as the pioneer log cabin. In the Hudson Valley the Dutch settlers retained their preference for brick and stone, while in Florida, Texas, and later in California, Spanish influences were strongly felt.

By the beginning of the eighteenth century, however, Britain had gained control over the whole of the eastern coastline of what is now the United States. Architects began to arrive, full of enthusiasm for the new mode of building which was gaining popularity at home. The Georgian style, England's belated response to the Renaissance, became firmly established in America, and remained dominant for a hundred years.

The English Georgian house was characterized by a simple rectangular shape, enlivened by the well-judged proportions of its window openings rather than any lavish use of ornamentation. In town, middle-class homes were tall and narrow, often rearing to four or five storeys on a frontage of as little as 24 feet (7·3 m.), but, because of their arrangement in long terraces, a top-heavy effect was avoided. A group of houses, treated as an architectural entity, could give the impression of a large mansion. The Georgian style gave English towns some of their most beautiful streets, before it eventually succumbed to the nineteenth-century taste for the gothic.

Building standards improved after about 1700, as the innovations of the seventeenth century became the accepted practice of the eighteenth. The

An American pioneer's log cabin.

Georgian houses in Bedford Square, London.

greater availability of bricks made timber-framed houses obsolete in England, while the newly invented dog-legged stairs, two parallel flights separated by an inter-floor half-landing, took up less space than the older forms of staircase. One introduction, however, was of less obvious benefit. Sliding sash windows, which probably originated in Holland, were imported into England in the last quarter of the seventeenth century. Within a short time they were in such vogue that no self-respecting house could be without them. The tall sash window became an essential feature of Georgian house design, and the less draughty, hinged casement was not revived until the very end of the era.

A middle-class English town family of Georgian times could expect to live in comfort. Servants were easy to come by, and raised no objections to working in dimly lit basement kitchens and sleeping in tiny attic bedrooms. Sandwiched between these twin domains of the servants were the main rooms of the house—tall, airy, and well supplied with fireplaces to keep the winter cold at bay. The only major inadequacies were the lack of effective sanitation and the doubtful nature of the water supply.

Unfortunately the standards of city life showed no improvements for the poor. As towns grew more crowded during the eighteenth century, the price of building land increased, so that it became steadily more expensive to own or rent an entire house. People were driven into tenements made by the division of decaying properties into flats or even single rooms. In England, where the tradition of the one-family house was strong, this was felt as a great hardship. On the Continent and in Scotland, however, flat-dwelling, so repugnant to the English, was already well established. The early seventeenth-century stone-built tenements of Edinburgh, which were higher than any contemporary houses in London, were designed for multi-family occupation. Staircases were shared by everyone; home was generally no more than two rooms on the same level.

The steady trickle of people attracted to the towns became a torrent as the Industrial Revolution burst, first on England and then on the rest of the western world. British industry had been gathering strength throughout the eighteenth century, but while water remained the main source of power its impact was limited. Factories were often located in remote river valleys,

A seventeenth-century tenement in Lawnmarket, Edinburgh.

and the houses provided by the employers had to be reasonably comfortable to attract and hold workers. It was only after 1800, when steam engines were put to work in large numbers, that factories became concentrated around the canals and coalfields, and encroached, in a big way, on existing towns. The effect on parts of England was devastating. Towns mushroomed at a time when the Napoleonic Wars had increased the cost of both labour and building materials. Row on row of shoddy terrace houses were erected by speculative builders, using the poorest quality bricks obtainable. Walls were sometimes only the thickness of one brick; foundations were omitted; often ground floors were no more than beaten earth. Whole blocks were known to tumble about their inmates' ears. Faulty construction was not the only hazard. Sanitation varied from primitive to non-existent, and the new working-class districts were converted into disease-infested swamps. The very word 'slum', which was first coined in the 1820s, was derived from 'slump', an old country expression meaning 'bog'.

But even at their worst, with grim gardenless houses standing back-to-back, the new terraces did offer each family a home of its own. Many industrial workers were far more poorly housed. Building could not keep up with the demand for accommodation, and people were forced to accept appalling conditions. Home for many was no more than a share in a crowded tenement room. A family with a whole room to itself was considered fortunate. Even windowless, waterlogged cellars were pressed into use. In the early nineteenth century up to a sixth of the population of Liverpool lived below ground.

As industrialization spread to new countries similar conditions appeared abroad. The nineteenth century was marked by an unprecedented growth of cities in Europe and America; the twentieth century has seen this process extended to the whole world. In the twenty years from 1820 to 1840, when the city population of the United States trebled, existing houses were divided up into tenements which rapidly deteriorated into slums. This pattern of uncontrolled growth and falling standards has been repeated time and time again.

However, the picture has not been entirely black. Industrial squalor produced a reaction, first in Britain and then in other countries. Governments, local authorities, and charitable individuals have all worked to bring about better conditions, while laws have been enacted to ensure that building standards improved. After 1875 no British builder was allowed to erect town houses lacking piped water, a patch of garden, and at least one window to each room. The bye-law houses built to comply with the minimum requirements of these regulations still flank many back streets in industrial

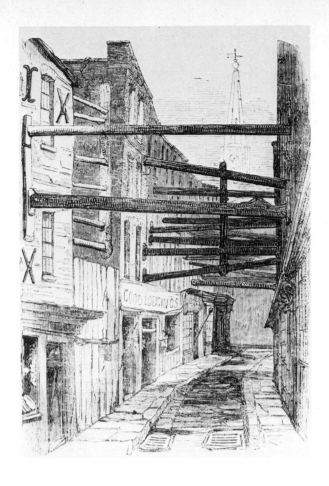

Working-class housing in mid-nineteenth-century London.

towns. Their monotonous serried ranks seem an affront to human individuality, but nevertheless they represent a real advance in working-class housing.

Technical progress also held out the promise of better living conditions. During the nineteenth century the well-to-do learnt to regard piped water, flushing lavatories, and purpose-built bathrooms as part and parcel of a civilized life. In the twentieth century the luxuries of the few have become the necessities of the many. Gas and electricity have given new possibilities for heating and lighting. People's expectations have increased, and so, correspondingly, has the dissatisfaction of those condemned to dwell in slum tenements.

The nineteenth century has left the industrial countries of the West with a residue of sub-standard housing that they have still to eradicate. New, developing lands are faced with the even bigger problem of the influx of peasants into already over-extended towns. Many Asian and Latin American cities are ringed by squatters' encampments of depressing squalor. High-rise 29

flats, towers of concrete, steel, and glass, provide a partial solution. They rise, gleaming and clinical, in all the continents of the world—an international response to the pressure on urban accommodation. But still there is never enough new building to cope with demand, and the flats themselves while easing some problems create others. Many people find it so difficult to live with the sheer scale of the tower block that, for all the new-found and much appreciated amenities, they miss the neighbourliness of their former slum homes. Mothers with young families complain that there is nowhere for the children to play; the elderly feel isolated; teenagers become alienated by the anonymity of their surroundings and resort to vandalism. Although long tradition has accustomed some Scottish and Continental townsmen to flat dwelling, the majority of people still dream of a house and garden of their own. Unfortunately it seems impossible to reconcile this understandable longing with the need to limit the further encroachment of town on country. Coveted suburban villas are for the prosperous. On an international level inequalities are even more dangerous. Rapid communication is shrinking the world, awaking people to its painful contrasts. The traditional dwelling no longer seems adequate to the villager who has once experienced the plumbing, air conditioning, and electric power of the great city. Man has the capacity to make more luxurious shelters than ever before, but is overwhelmed by the scale of demand.

2

Home Cooking

Chinese cooking may pre-date all other cuisines. The earliest man-made
fires were lit 360,000 years ago in caves near modern Peking and the
discovery of cooking probably followed quite quickly. Meat stored near the
fire would have been found improved in flavour and texture, and what began
as an accident would have grown into a custom.

At first cooking must have been limited to roasting, with the joint placed
at the edge or even on the fire, but gradually better techniques evolved.
Meat skewered on a pointed stick could be held clear of the ashes, while
fire-heated stones could be used as the equivalent of modern hot plates.
Hot stones have been used by primitive peoples well into historical times.
When Charles Darwin visited Tahiti in the 1830s he found that the inhabitants wrapped their food in leaves and placed it between two layers of hot
stones which were then heaped with earth to slow down cooling. Another
people, the Bushmen of southern Africa, used heated stones in a different
way. Until very recent times they boiled their food by dropping hot stones
into a bladder or skin containing water. Probably, at least some early
Stone Age societies practised similar methods, but there is no certain evidence
that meat was boiled before the invention of pottery.

Pottery was a by-product of the neolithic agricultural revolution, which
took place 10,000 years ago in the Middle East. In those days the climate
was damper than at present and many of what are now arid zones were well-
watered and fertile. Under these favourable conditions scattered bands of
food gatherers began hesitantly to plant their own crops rather than search
for wild fruits and vegetables. Settled village life began and the produce
of one harvest was saved to eke out existence until the next. This new way
of life demanded better storage facilities and the early farmers seem to
have invented pottery to supplement woven baskets and scooped-out stone
bowls. But however the pot came into existence, it must have proved a boon
for the cook. At last it became possible to prepare food without contaminating
32 it with ashes, earth or soot. A whole new range of culinary opportunity must

Kitchen scene from wall painting in tomb of Rameses III, twelfth century B.C.

have opened up.

With the advent of farming villages and permanent houses came the first of what can properly be called kitchens in the modern sense. In Jericho, a very early farming settlement, the bee-hive shaped huts of the original inhabitants had given way to larger, rectangular houses by about 6800 B.C. These usually consisted of several rooms grouped around a courtyard which contained a hearth for cooking.

The Jericho housewife could cook alfresco for most days in the year without discomfort, but it was a different story at another neolithic site of comparable antiquity lying well to the north in the Turkish uplands. Here excavations on the ancient mound of Çatal Hüyük have revealed a strange town of interlocking, box-like houses which presented completely blank walls to the outside world. There was not a single door or window for an enemy or flood water to penetrate—instead each house was entered from a hole in the roof. The kitchen area, with its hearth, lay just below the opening which thus served as door, window and chimney. Some housewives of Çatal Hüyük had a clay oven as well as an open hearth and so could bake bread as well as roast or boil. Earthenware cooking pots appeared in this community around 6500 B.C.

The kitchen could not advance much beyond the stage achieved at Çatal Hüyük until men had learnt to work with metals and fashion virtually fire-proof utensils. During the third millennium B.C. bronze came into fairly large-scale use in Mesopotamia. Egypt, which lacked tin to mix with its copper, trailed behind, but by the second millennium it too had moved

33

into the Bronze Age. The tools of the cook's trade began to multiply.

Wall paintings in the tomb of the Pharaoh Rameses III, who died in 1151 B.C., show animated scenes from the royal kitchens. Some servants pound ingredients in large mortars, others tend a great metal cauldron boiling over a fire, cooks twirl a sort of macaroni in a heated pan, bakers dance in a trough of dough kneading it with their feet, scullions flit hither and thither carrying loaded pots or bearing trays of cakes on their heads. The great variety and profusion of kitchen equipment is at once apparent. There are pots and shallow pans over open fires, closed ovens for baking, work tables for the pastry cooks, troughs, basins, and storage jars by the dozen. Ropes passing through rings in the ceiling support trays of food out of the reach of prowling rats and clear of the bustle below.

Pictures of less exalted kitchens appear in the tombs of some Egyptian noblemen. From these it seems that the magoor, a sort of charcoal brazier still used in the remoter villages of the Nile Valley today, was employed by the cooks in ancient times to keep their stews simmering. The method of roasting a goose is also illustrated. The cook crouched beside an open hearth holding the bird on a spit with one hand while waving a fan over the fire with the other.

Ordinary Egyptians, of course, made do with far less equipment than was featured in the well-stocked kitchens of the Pharaoh or nobles. Cooking and food preparation were often carried out in the courtyard of the peasant's house. Here barley grain might be ground into flour in a hand-mill, worked into a dough, and finally baked in a crude oven. The Egyptian oven consisted initially of an enclosure formed by a large flat stone resting on two or three others. Wood was poked into the oven and set alight. When the stones were not enough, the fire was allowed to burn down, the ashes were quickly raked out, and the small, round loaves were introduced, to bake in the stored heat. Brick-built ovens were used in the kitchens of large Egyptian households from about 2000 B.C., but probably the poorer people stuck to their make-shift arrangements much longer.

The Mesopotamian civilization, which flourished at the same time as the Egyptian, has left behind no colourful paintings of kitchen scenes. There are a few carvings of cooks tending charcoal braziers, but if it were not for the direct evidence of the archaeologist's spade little would be known of the kitchens in which they worked. All the famous middle-class dwellings of the early second millennium B.C. excavated at Ur possessed a special room set aside for cooking purposes. Typically this lay behind the stairs leading up to a second storey and possessed a stone flour grinder, still in position, as well as a cooking range.

Ancient clay model of Egyptian fanning a kitchen fire.

The less elaborate houses of a thousand or more years later, investigated at Babylon, lacked an upper storey but all could still boast a separate kitchen with a fireplace in one corner. This ingenious hearth consisted of two low brick piers, started six inches apart at ground level and brought closer together with each succeeding course until only a narrow slit remained between them at the top. Charcoal or dried wood was burnt in the gap between the piers, and cooking pots were placed over the slit to heat. Storage facilities were not neglected. Most Babylonian kitchens of this period possessed a terracotta chest where food could be stored safe from the depredations of rats and mice. Somewhere near at hand there would also be a stand for the jars of water which every day were carried up from the river.

The Middle East had been the centre of man's progress for many thousands of years. It had fostered the Agricultural Revolution, seen the invention of pottery, and led the way in the introduction of metals. To the resourcefulness of its peoples, the cook owed not only the wide variety of foods available for his pot, but also the very utensils of his trade. Nearly everything in the kitchen, except for the fire in the hearth, owed its origin to the Middle East. At last, however, the centre of civilization began to move towards the west, and Greece and Rome rose to greatness.

Greek houses remained remarkably plain and simple until the conquests of Alexander the Great (356–323 B.C.) undermined the independence of the old city-states and ushered in the more luxurious Hellenistic Age. While the cities retained their power Greek energies were focused on public affairs, and private ostentation was rare. Kitchens, like the houses themselves, were functional almost to the point of primitiveness. Cooking, in fact, must often have been carried out in the open courtyard, since in a play written by Menander (342–291 B.C.) a hired cook is made to ask whether a prospective employer's kitchen has a roof. The view that many Greek houses had no special room set aside for cooking and food preparation is supported by

An early Greek oven.

a fragment surviving from the works of Alexis, another fourth-century playwright, in which a character enquires: 'Boy, is there a kitchen?' To the modern mind the lack of a kitchen might seem an almost incredible hardship, but the inconvenience would have been much more apparent than real. The Greeks often cooked over a small, portable hearth, and what could be more sensible than to carry this out into the courtyard on a warm, pleasant day? If the weather were less kind the hearth could easily be taken indoors and placed near a window so that the fumes from the fire could escape. But fixed kitchens did, of course, exist. The fifth- and fourth-century houses excavated on the site of the northern city of Olynthus contained tiny kitchens with permanent hearths. Only the lower parts of the walls of these dwellings remained, but some authorities feel confident that the kitchen ceiling was carried upwards to terminate in a sort of flue through which smoke and cooking smells could vent.

The Roman world, of which Greece eventually became a part, encompassed the entire Mediterranean, and at its greatest extent stretched from the Caspian Sea in the east to Britain in the north and Spain in the west. Within this vast territory there existed such sharp contrasts in climate and cultural background that although the Romans successfully imposed their architectural ideas on official buildings throughout the empire, they made little impact on the homes of ordinary men and women outside the towns. The wealthy, of course, aped Roman ways and built themselves Italian-style country villas and city houses, but the peasantry continued to live in whatever sort of dwelling had been traditional before the conqueror's arrival. Kitchens were as varied as the houses they served.

In Rome itself the majority of the people lived in tiny flats with no means of heating or cooking other than charcoal-fired braziers whose fumes had to find their way out as best they could through open windows. Some braziers had hollow sides or receptacles in which water could be heated, while others were fitted with bars for grilling and rings to take pots and pans. Despite these refinements, cooking must have been an onerous chore for the average Roman housewife, but perhaps the problem of washing up was even more serious. Although Rome had many fine aqueducts none of the flats had running water, so that every drop required had to be carried up the stairs. No wonder the numerous cook-shops of the capital never lacked customers.

Wealthy Romans, with their love of high living and sumptuous banquets, could not afford to ignore the needs of their cooks. Each mansion had a properly designed kitchen tucked away at the rear, often small but always well equipped and sometimes even decorated with frescoes. The hearth was simple but effective. Small charcoal fires, one for each pot, were lit on top of a brick or masonry platform, which was raised to a convenient height for the cook. Some hearths had plain, flat tops, but others were crowned by a series of brick-built cells intended to contain the individual fires. The illustration shows a kitchen range of this sort found at Pompeii. Here the cells were rectangular and left open at the front so that the ashes could be easily removed. The brick sides served to support the gridirons and tripods on which the cooking utensils were stood. A reserve of fuel was kept dry and ready to hand in the cupboard in the hearth-platform itself. Sensible design

A Roman cauldron.

A Roman cooking range found in the ruins of Pompeii.

made the Roman hearth easy and economical to use but the problem of what to do with fumes from the fire was never satisfactorily solved. About the best that the cook could expect was a hole in the wall through which some of the smoke might escape. Reasonable washing-up facilities were, however, provided in these better-class homes, and many kitchen sinks have been discovered amongst the ruins of Pompeii. There was also no shortage of utensils. The kitchen in a wealthy establishment was well stocked with kettles, pans, ladles, sieves, funnels, mortars, spoons, and knives, as well as all manner of pots and dishes. Strangely enough though, the Romans, despite their knowledge of the trident, do not seem to have used the fork for either cooking or eating purposes.

In Britain, one of the least civilized regions of the empire, Roman culture was only skin deep. Though the southern parts of the province had their share of villas, the typical Briton of those times still lived in a round, thatch-roofed hut heated by a central hearth. Cooking was usually done around this domestic fire, but in some of the larger dwellings food was prepared in out-house kitchens. Equipment varied with the wealth of the household. The kitchen of a prosperous farmer might contain a large bronze cauldron with an iron tripod to support it, all manner of pottery basins, plates, dishes, and strainers, metal chopping knives and pot-hooks, and numerous wooden spoons, cups, and bowls. A poor family, on the other hand, probably made do with a few earthenware cooking pots, plain wooden platters and cups, and the bare minimum of knives and wooden spoons.

During the Saxon raids of the fourth century and invasions of the fifth, towns and villas were sacked or simply left to fall into decay. Britain lost its veneer of civilization and the good life enjoyed by the privileged few became impossible. By and large, however, the domestic comforts of a Saxon farmer could have been little, if at all, inferior to those of the British peasant he displaced. Most people probably continued to cook by the hearth which warmed their hut, and although the Saxon sometimes dug additional fire-pits outside his home, perhaps for use in summer or when preparing a particularly large meal, Asser's famous story of how King Alfred burnt the cakes leaves little doubt that indoor cooking was the normal practice. To possess a separate kitchen was, however, such an unusual mark of wealth and distinction that an eleventh-century document lists it as one of the requirements for recognition as a nobleman.

The Saxon invasions of Britain were just one symptom of the collapse of Roman power. All over Europe the barbarians had swept in, destroying, plundering, and setting up petty kingdoms. Towns dependent on trade could not prosper in such unsettled times. Urban populations melted away and with them were lost all the domestic niceties of the Roman civilization. The bath, central heating, and the neat, well-contrived kitchen became things of the past.

After the eleventh century standards of comfort began very slowly to improve. The purpose-built kitchen became less of a rarity and, perhaps because of the fire risk, even some relatively humble households did their cooking in outhouses. In England, however, such refinements did not extend to the agricultural labourer whose cottage, right up to the close of the medieval era, consisted of just one earthen-floored room. The peasant's kitchen was the open air in summer and a fire kindled in the middle of the floor during the winter. In fact, if the evidence of the Bayeux Tapestry is anything to go by, some of the poorest people may have cooked out of doors all year round, for there is no sign of a smoke-hole in any of the tiny cottages depicted.

The detached kitchens of even the largest houses were initially very flimsy

In the Middle Ages much cooking took place out of doors. This illustration is taken from a fourteenth-century manuscript.

structures—often nothing more than wooden laths and plaster. Royalty built no better than its subjects, and in 1232 the kitchen of Henry III's Oxford residence was brought crashing down during a storm. Wooden buildings of this sort were far too subject to the ravages of weather and fire for any to have survived into modern times, so most of what is known of them is due to the science of archaeology. Generally it seems the kitchens of this period were square in shape with the fireplace built in the centre to keep the flames well away from inflammable walls. Outdoor hearths are often found close to the kitchen and there can be little doubt that given a fine day even the cooks of these more exalted households preferred to work in the cool of the open air. Several pictures from contemporary manuscripts show scenes which support this view.

The old Saxon nobility of England had relied as heavily on wood for its domestic architecture as the common people. After the Norman Conquest the picture slowly began to change, and stone was used not only for churches and castles but also in the construction of the private houses of the wealthy. Eventually the fashion spread to embrace even the kitchen, as the splendid, fourteenth-century example at Glastonbury Abbey still shows. With the adoption of stone, the need for a central hearth vanished, and wall fireplaces could be introduced. Externally the Glastonbury kitchen is square, but on the inside its builders have made it into an octagon by placing a fireplace across each of the four corners. Flues conducted the smoke from the fires upwards to vent through proper chimney shafts. At last the kitchen was freed from the nuisance of smoke and fumes drifting up from a central

For fear of fire, medieval kitchens were often detached from the buildings they served. This illustration shows the kitchen at the Abbey of Fontevrault, built late in the twelfth century.

The medieval kitchen of Windsor Palace as it appeared early in the nineteenth century.

hearth to a louver in the roof, and cooks must have been much less tempted than before to carry their pots and pans out of doors.

Large medieval kitchens were provided with a formidable array of utensils. A twelfth-century vocabulary mentions chopping tables, pots, tripods, axes, mortars and pestles, pot-sticks, pot-hooks, cauldrons, frying-pans, gridirons, saucepans, dishes, platters, vessels for mixing sauce, hand-mills, pepper-mills, and mills for making breadcrumbs. Of the actual cooking vessels the cauldron was undoubtedly the most frequently used. Livestock was not generally kept through the winter when fodder was in short supply; instead animals were slaughtered in autumn and salted down. As a result salt meat, best cooked by boiling in the cauldron, formed a common item of diet, while fresh meat suitable for roasting was a comparative luxury during most of the year even in noble households. Usually the cauldron stood on a separate tripod, but sometimes, especially after about 1400, it was hung from a hook and ratchet device which enabled its height above the fire to be easily adjusted. Cauldron-cooking had a particular advantage for the scullions. It could supply uncontaminated hot water for washing up, provided the joint were first sealed in an earthenware pot with a watertight covering. Copious hot water must have been very necessary in getting the   41

This copy of a fifteenth-century painting shows the pot-hook used to adjust the height of a cooking pot above the fire.

dishes clean, since the only other aid was a mixture of linseed oil and wood ash with a little sand added to give abrasion.

Poultry and game and fresh meat when available were often roasted, though even these sometimes found their way into the cauldron. The medieval method of roasting involved impaling the carcass or joint on a spit, which was supported in front of an open fire and slowly turned to ensure even cooking. Initially spits were no more than plain wooden stakes, but gradually it became customary to use iron and to fit a handle for ease of turning. Andirons were often provided with brackets into which spits could be fitted. The illustration, based on a painting in a fifteenth-century manuscript bible, shows just such as arrangement.

As long as the kitchen employed a central hearth, the baking oven had to be a free-standing affair made of stone or clay. With the advent of the wall fireplace, however, came the possibility of integrating the oven into the main structure of the building. In the Abbot's kitchen at Glastonbury, for example, an oven has been let into the thickness of the wall behind one of the fireplaces. There was nothing elaborate about the medieval oven. It consisted simply of a stone-lined space, usually provided with some kind of door which could be shut to help retain the heat. A wood fire was kindled inside, and when the temperature had risen sufficiently, all the ashes were raked out. The pasties, dough, and the like which were to be baked were then introduced on the end of a long-handled shovel of the sort used by bakers to this day. Once the door was shut, baking could proceed using the heat stored in the surrounding stones.

A medieval turnspit roasting a joint.

Despite the simplicity of its design the oven remained a luxury enjoyed by relatively few. The flimsy hut of the peasant or the poor townsman contained no wall capable of holding an oven, and most people baked on a flat stone set in front of the fire. To off-set this difficulty some municipalities provided public ovens for their citizens, but professional bakers, who were prepared to cook pies and pasties brought in by customers as well as bake their own bread, were also active from an early date.

By the close of the Middle Ages changes in the style and size of domestic buildings began to affect cooking arrangements. Noblemen had learnt that food arrived warmer at table if the cooks were provided with facilities inside the main house, and after 1500 the isolated kitchen became increasingly old-fashioned. Ordinary people could still not afford to set aside a special room as kitchen, but as their homes grew larger and more substantial they could at least hope to incorporate a simple oven, little more than a brick-lined hole, into the structure of the hall fireplace. To make an oven of 43 reasonable size the wall at this point was often thickened to give a domed bulge on the outside. These can still be noticed in many old cottages, even when the original ovens have long since been bricked in.

But apart from this spread in the use of the oven, the early Tudor kitchen could display little that was positively new. The cauldron remained much in evidence; roasting was still done on a spit in front of an open fire; even the oven was heated in medieval fashion. Changes were mainly in matters of detail. Andirons, for instance, now not only possessed brackets to support roasting-spits, but were often broadened out at the top into hobs on which saucepans could be placed to simmer. In the kitchens of some great houses, however, an early labour-saving device had made its appearance. The old manually operated roasting-spits were increasingly replaced by those worked by machinery.

Spit-turning machines seem to have originated on the Continent where several different varieties developed. The oldest was probably the so-called 'smoke jack' which was worked from pulleys, attached to a fan in the chimney. One ancient German picture seems to put this device well back into medieval times, but if in use at such an early date it must certainly have been a rarity. It was not until the sixteenth century that travellers to Switzerland and Germany began to make frequent mention of the smoke jacks used in some of the larger inns. The idea was imported to England, but although the device was occasionally employed here in the seventeenth century—the diarist John Evelyn mentions one in his brother's house—it did not enjoy any great popularity for another hundred years. The smoke jack, for all its ingenuity, suffered from one serious drawback. To work properly it required a strong chimney draught, and cooks were sometimes tempted to stoke up the kitchen fire just to keep the spit turning.

Waste of this kind was avoided by the weight- or spring-driven spits which so impressed the French writer Montaigne with their novelty during his visit to Switzerland in 1580. He attributed their widespread use to the Swiss being 'such excellent smiths', but even in comparatively backward England similar devices could be found. The roasting-spits in the kitchen at Hampton Court were operated by the fall of a heavy weight which was cranked up by a handle before cooking began. Clockwork spits were also known in Italy during the sixteenth century if not earlier. Leonardo da Vinci (1452–1519) seems to have been fully conversant with mechanically driven spits, for he suggested one powered by a primitive steam turbine.

The existence of all these machines makes the exploitation of animal turn-spits seem even less excusable. Be this as it may many English kitchens, from Tudor times right up to the eighteenth century, employed an un-

Dogs were still sometimes used as turnspits in eighteenth-century Britain. This scene in a Welsh inn kitchen was recorded by Thomas Rowlandson during a tour in 1797.

fortunate dog, confined in a sort of squirrel-cage, to keep the roast turning. The dog had to maintain an incessant trot, and if his efforts showed signs of flagging, a hot ember from the fire was applied to his heels. There was, however, a very simple alternative to both dog and machine, which even the great Dr. Johnson was not ashamed to use. In common with what was probably the vast majority of poorer people he suspended his joint of meat in front of the fire on a twisted string.

Mechanical turn-spits deserve a detailed consideration as the first major effort to reduce the physical labour involved in cooking, but other innovations were perhaps ultimately more important in the evolution of the modern kitchen. One such change was triggered by the emergence during the fifteenth century of a self-conscious middle class anxious to isolate itself from its social inferiors. The well-to-do burgher no longer felt it fitting that the servants should prepare meals in his presence. To avoid this affront to his dignity the house was modified by converting one of the rooms adjoining the hall into a kitchen. By the seventeenth century, when this process was fairly complete, it was only in the houses of the poor that the living-room fire still doubled as a cooking hearth. The kitchen was now firmly established as a specialized utility room.

The seventeenth century also saw the beginning of a new line of development in kitchen fireplaces. Limited improvements had already been made with the still-dominant wood-burning fire—basket spits, for instance, had made it easier to roast large pieces of meat—but much more profound changes were to flow from the gradual adoption of coal as the basic British household fuel. The old-fashioned flat hearth, on which the logs had rested

45

Poor people often suspended their roasting joint in front of the fire at the end of a twisted string. Cartoon drawn by James Gillray in 1787.

with their ends propped up on andirons or firedogs, was not suitable for burning coal, and an entirely different sort of grate had to be devised with a raised fire-box made out of iron bars. Given the right conditions, however, coal could burn much more fiercely than wood. For the cook this carried mixed blessings. All her dishes cooked more quickly, but her methods had to be adapted to a more concentrated form of heat.

As early as 1670 more Londoners burnt coal than wood, but particularly in the country where logs remained cheap, some women resisted the innovation, preferring to work by the cleaner, if slower fuel. But inexorably, as England's forests dwindled, coal gained ground. By the early eighteenth century most kitchens in the larger towns of England were equipped with an open coal fire for roasting and boiling, though baking was still done in the traditional brick oven heated by brushwood or faggots. It was, however, only a matter of time before the ironwork made necessary by the use of coal was extended to provide a more convenient arrangement for the cook. The first step in this process was the hob grate in which a metal box was placed on either side of the fire, narrowing down the hearth and giving two hot-plates on which pots could be set to simmer. It took longer to incorporate the oven into the structure of the kitchen fire, but in 1769 Hornbuckle suggested that to serve this purpose an iron box might be fitted behind the grate. A more practicable design originated with Thomas Robinson who in 1780 took out a patent for a cast-iron range with an oven on one side. Three years later Langmead introduced a further refinement when he patented a kitchen fireplace with an oven on one side and a boiler for heating water on the other. A basic pattern had been set that in England at least was to persist for a century.

The early kitchen range was, however, a large and expensive item, made to the customer's order and quite beyond the means of any but the well-to-do. Worse still it was incredibly extravagant in its use of coal, having an immensely wide open fire with only tiny ovens at its sides. Sir Benjamin Thompson, better known by his Germanic title of Count Rumford, was horrified by such prodigality. The English, he wrote during a visit in the 1790s, consumed more fuel 'to boil a tea-kettle than with proper management would suffice to cook a meal for fifty men'. His main criticism was aimed at the wastefulness of the attempt 'to heat ovens and boilers by heat drawn off laterally from a fire in an open grate'. Rumford was speaking with authority. During his eleven-year period as a high official in the Bavarian administration he had already achieved remarkable fuel economies by his modifications to the workhouse kitchen in the state capital of Munich. This success was followed by the construction of several kitchens in Britain itself, where he installed cooking apparatus in a number of private homes and public institutions.

Rumford's scientifically designed kitchen range consisted not of a single large open fireplace but numerous small ones, built into a raised counter and each closed off at the top by a cooking vessel which lowered flush into the circular fire opening so as to leave only lid and handle visible above. In this way the saucepan was literally bathed in hot air and was able to absorb heat through its sides as well as its bottom. The only serious heat losses were upwards, and these were reduced by making the lid double-walled with an insulating layer of air trapped between the surfaces. This

In the 1790s Count Rumford designed kitchen ranges of almost incredible efficiency.

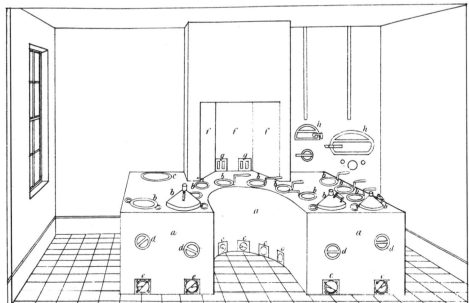

was not all. Before the smoke from whatever fires happened to be alight was allowed to escape up the chimney, it was milked of all further usable heat by being passed through a series of flues surrounding either a hot-water boiler or an oven. Oven roasting, Rumford had discovered, could give just as good results as the spit. To complete the economy the cook was under strict instructions to light only those fires which were absolutely necessary.

Given the technology of the day, Rumford's range was as near perfection as could be achieved. Perhaps, in fact, it was too perfect, with an attention to detail which seemed unrealistic in the workaday world. For, whatever the reason, Rumford's ideas were only slowly or partially accepted. Roasting in a closed oven did not gain any great currency in England until the mid-nineteenth century, while separate fires for each pot had to wait on the development of the gas cooker. His example did, however, lead to the introduction of the kitchener in which a metal plate closed off the top of the fire.

The first fireplace of this kind was designed by George Bodley in 1802. Its iron top served as a hotplate, while a flue passed under and round an oven at the side. The hot gases from the fire were thus denied access to the chimney until they had given up some of their heat. Here, however, the similarity to Rumford's ideas ended. Bodley's fire had an open front, presumably for roasting, and the oven, which was lined with fire-bricks, was intended merely for baking.

Despite Rumford's advocacy and Bodley's pioneering the closed kitchen fireplace did not gain popularity quickly. The open range had already established a favourable reputation and was, by the early years of the nineteenth century, in full commercial production. It was not until the 1830s that the kitchener emerged as a serious rival. For the rest of the nineteenth century both types of grate developed side-by-side, the open variety retaining its greatest hold in the northern mining counties where coal was cheap. The monstrous coal-fired range, voracious in its appetite, spewing dust and soot, and demanding a daily libation of blacklead, became the veritable god of the middle-class Victorian kitchen, worshipped and feared by generations of kitchen-maids.

Working-class housewives were slower to adopt the kitchen range. Not that they would have disagreed with the author of *The English Housekeeper* who wrote in 1842 that she knew 'of no apparatus so desirable as the common kitchen range . . . which has a boiler for hot water, on one side, and an oven on the other. . . .' It was rather that they often lived, cooked, and slept in one room, so that if poverty did not forbid such a luxury, lack of space did. As the nineteenth century progressed, however, various less expensive

Mid-nineteenth-century kitchen.

cooking aids came on to the market. One widely used in kitchens of all sorts was a roasting screen made from a curved sheet of polished metal with a trough for dripping below. The screen was pushed up close to the firebars and the joint was hung vertically in the space between, either on the end of a piece of twisted string or, if the cook possessed such a thing, from a so-called 'bottle-jack'. The bottle-jack was a clockwork device which rotated the joint first one way and then the other about a vertical axis. It was invented about 1820 as an alternative to the horizontal spit.

But much more important technical developments were on the way, which were eventually to transform the kitchens of the entire nation and end the long reliance on solid fuel. Ever since gas had first been manufactured commercially for lighting purposes in 1812, sporadic attempts had been made to harness its heating properties. Over the years several experimenters achieved limited success with installations in their own homes, but it was not until the 1840s and 1850s that gas cookers began to come on to the open market. Amongst the pioneers of this time were Charles Rickets, whose cooker was advertised in the *Journal of Gas Lighting* in 1849, Alfred King, whose surprisingly modern-looking designs were in production in 1850, and James Sharp and Ebenezer Goddard, both of whom exhibited at a display of gas cooking stoves held at London's Polytechnic Institution in 1851. All this flurry of activity, however, was premature. Despite the enthusiastic support of the famous French chef Alexis Soyer, who created a stir in 1850 by successfully roasting a whole ox over a home-made gas range, the public remained deeply distrustful. A few restaurants and hotels began to cook by

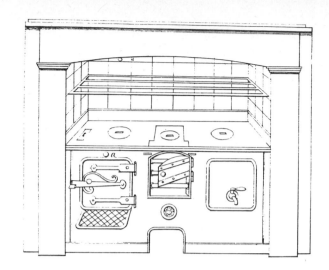

Solid-fuel kitchen range, 1869.

A gas cooker manufactured by Alfred King in 1859.

gas, but hardly any sales were made to ordinary householders. Writing some years later Alfred King had sadly to admit that 'the manufacturers who had embarked in the business found it either impossible or unwise to continue it'.

The set-back was considerable but the advantages of a source of heat which could be turned on or off with a flick of the wrist could not be permanently ignored. Later inventors also possessed an advantage denied their predecessors. The advent of the Bunsen burner in 1855 made it possible to burn gas efficiently and avoid sooty deposits. By the late 1870s the gas cooker was beginning to win a grudging acceptance, though as late as 1889 an American manufacturer thought it advisable to mention in his catalogue that 'popular prejudice (was) gradually giving way'. The breakthrough in Britain came in that very same year, with the introduction of the coin-in-the-slot meter. This, together with the spreading practice amongst supply companies of renting out cookers, did much to popularize gas cooking.

Universal *gas cooker, about 1886.*

Improvements in design also played their part. According to the *Cooking Appliance Report* of the 1880 Glasgow Exhibition of Lighting and Heating Appliances, the prejudice against gas had been due in large measure to 'the peculiar and unsavoury gas flavour imparted to food by earlier stoves'. After concluding that this fault was due to defective burners and lack of ventilation in the ovens, the report went on to claim that such points were 'now attended to by all manufacturers worthy of the name'. In the decade that followed efficiency was further enhanced by a much more general acceptance by manufacturers of the need for oven lagging. Designs, however, were still far from perfect. The gas cooker of 1890 was a large and rather ugly contrivance, drab black in colour, and very difficult to clean because of lack of access. The latter defect was cured in 1891 by the Richmond Company's introduction of a cooker with removable burners, but appearance showed little improvement until 1910 when white enamel began to replace black on range tops and splash backs. In 1915 an oven thermostat was produced by the American Stove Company, giving cooks an entirely new precision of control. By the 1920s the gas cooker had developed to the point where it not only scored in convenience but was actually cheaper to run than a coal-burning range.

The success of gas created a climate of public opinion ready to accept other new modes of cooking. Within a few years of the opening of the first commercial generating station in 1881, strenuous efforts were being made to develop a reliable electric cooker. The early fruits of this research were shown at a display of electrical goods staged in 1891 at the Crystal Palace near London, and only two years later a complete 'Model Electric Kitchen', featuring kettles, range and broiler, all worked by electricity, was exhibited at the Chicago World's Fair. Further interest was engendered in 1896 by the promotion of an electrically cooked banquet in honour of the Lord Mayor of London. The prospects seemed promising, but there was still one great snag. All early cooking appliances encountered difficulty due to the rapid oxidation of the wires in their heating elements. It was not until highly resistant nickel-chromium alloys were discovered early in the twentieth century that really practicable electric cookers became possible. By 1905 several makes of cooker utilizing the new long-lasting wire were available. Electricity now entered what could be called its incubation period. Its advantages as a clean and flexible form of energy were well appreciated, but it was still expensive and its supply was limited to favoured areas. Teething troubles were also far from over. An article printed in a 1924 edition of the American journal *Electricity* makes this very clear with its complaint about 'excessive repair bills and the inconvenience connected

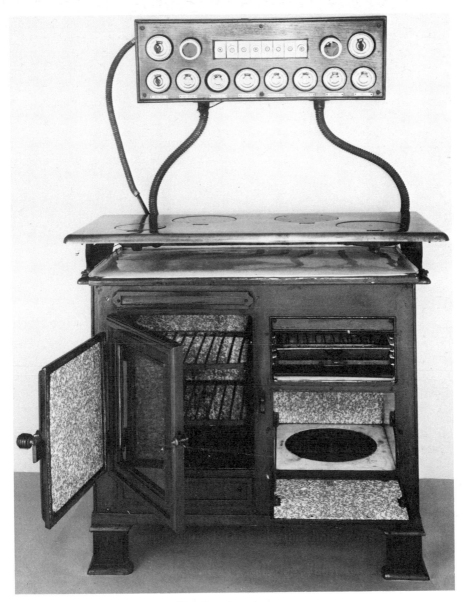

Electric cooker, about 1912.

with burning out of elements'. It was not until about 1930 that electricity emerged as a fully fledged rival to gas in the kitchen. Even today this rivalry continues and many housewives prefer the instant heat control which only gas cooking can give.

But electricity was not just a source of heat. It could be used for power as well, and inventors were quick to exploit its exciting possibilities. Electric washing machines were on sale in 1905 and vacuum cleaners followed in

Modern fitted kitchen.

1909. By 1917 an electrically driven domestic refrigerator had been perfected. The modern labour-saving home was on the way. Since the Second
World War electricity has found an ever-increasing application in the
kitchen. Automatic dish-washers, power mixers, and waste-disposal units
have all become popular. The United States has led the way in this movement, and even as long ago as 1950 had an estimated ten million mixers
in use.

Side-by-side with the development of these new tools have come improvements in the design of kitchen furniture. Laminated working surfaces and
gleaming wall cupboards have replaced the scrubbed wooden tables and
open dressers of former years. Bright sink units with stainless-steel tops have
helped reduced the drudgery of washing up. The modern kitchen manages
to combine efficiency with elegance, and reconcile technical innovation with
the practice of an age-old art.

3

Heating the Home

Once early man ventured out of his sun-baked African homeland and encountered harsher climates, fire became a necessity of life. It was no accident that the first people to live to the north of the frost line, the ancient inhabitants of the Choukoutien caves near modern Peking, possessed fire; they could not have survived without it.

The 360,000-year-old ashes found in these Chinese caverns prove Peking man's dominion over flame, but unfortunately provide no clue as to how his fire was obtained. Probably it was collected from natural outbreaks, and carefully tended to prevent it ever going out. The earliest evidence of complete mastery over fire comes from the cave of Krapina in Yugoslavia where a charred shaft of wood, which had clearly been twisted between the palms as a fire-stick, was discovered amongst remains dated to about 100,000 years ago.

In the thousand centuries which have passed since that fire-stick was thrown aside, mankind has emerged from the caves and learnt to build palaces and create civilizations. Metal has replaced stone; agriculture supplanted hunting; nation-states have taken over from family groupings. Change has affected nearly every facet of life, but in the matter of heating progress has been remarkably slow. The open fire is still in use today.

The world's first great civilizations grew up in Egypt and Mesopotamia where for much of the year the weather was hot. Houses in these lands were designed more to keep out the sun's rays than to fend off the chill of winter, but nevertheless, between November and March, nights and mornings could be unpleasantly cold. The answer to this occasional need for a fire was the portable brazier, which if used with charcoal as fuel caused little inconvenience from smoke. In wealthier Egyptian homes sweet-smelling materials were frequently burnt on the brazier to perfume the air of the room. Both Mesopotamian and Egyptian houses sometimes possessed permanent hearths, but these were often in the courtyard and were presumably employed for cooking. The illustration shows a copper brazier from Mesopotamia.

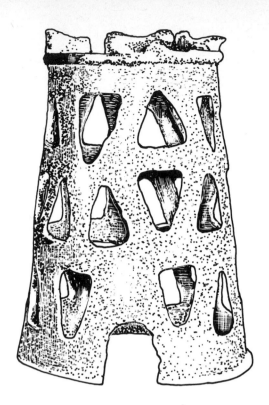

Sumerian brazier from the city of Nuzi.

Methods of domestic heating were little changed by the time of ancient Greece. It comes as no surprise to read in Homer's *Odyssey*, probably written in the eighth century B.C. when the Greeks were still half savage, of Penelope's maidservants plying braziers with fresh wood. What does come as a shock is to learn that some four hundred years later there was nothing better to warm the royal person of Alexander the Great. Plutarch tells of the king's displeasure when his host at an entertainment provided insufficient fuel for the brazier.

Although the Greeks seem to have relied heavily on portable fires, certain of their dwellings did possess fixed hearths as well. Excavations at Olynthus have revealed the existence of central fireplaces in the living-rooms of some fifth- and fourth-century houses. It is not known how the smoke from such fires escaped. Perhaps it merely made its way out through open windows and doors. Kitchen fires, however, sometimes boasted flues intended to carry away the fumes. Alexis, a poet active in the fourth century B.C., had one of his characters ask: 'Boy, is there a kitchen? Has it a chimney?' To which came the reply: 'Yes, but it is a bad one; the eyes will suffer.' Whether these kitchen flues were what we would today recognize as chimneys is open to question. They may have been little more than holes in the roof.

The Romans were the great heating engineers of antiquity, but it would be wrong to paint too glowing a picture of their domestic comfort. Although the rich did enjoy a limited form of central heating during Imperial times, the charcoal brazier remained the poor man's only means of heating right up to the collapse of the Western Empire. Even the mightiest, in fact, had sometimes to make do with its meagre warmth and risk its dangerous vapours. No less a person than the fourth-century emperor, Jovian, was suffocated by the fumes of a brazier set to warm his bedroom.

Roman braziers came in all sorts of shapes and sizes. Usually they consisted of an iron-lined hearth supported by a bronze stand, but although many were plain and workmanlike some were highly ornate, while others were designed to heat water as well as warm the room. One discovered at Pompeii had metal towers at each of the four corners of the shallow box which formed its hearth. When the hearth was piled with burning charcoal, water could be heated in the towers, but it is difficult to decide whether the intention was to humidify the air or to provide a supply of domestic hot water for the housewife. Perhaps it was a bit of both.

Under-floor heating was in use in the sweating chambers of Roman bath-houses during the first century B.C., but was apparently not applied to other

A Roman brazier which, besides warming a room, could heat small quantities of water.

The Roman hypocaust provided the rich with underfloor heating in some rooms.

rooms until the beginning of the Christian era. Seneca, about 4 B.C. to
A.D. 65, recorded that '. . . pipes from hypocausts, so inserted into the walls
as to spread an equal warmth through the room, and heat what are beneath
as well as what are above' were one of the innovations to come in during
his life-time.

The Roman hypocaust consisted essentially of a floor raised on brick
pillars so as to leave a space 2 or 3 feet (60–90 cm.) high through which smoke
and hot air from a furnace could circulate. Baked clay pipes set into the
walls rose from this under-floor cavity and opened into the upper rooms
through vents fitted with movable covers. These were probably closed whenever fresh fuel was applied, being re-opened to admit a current of hot air
only when the furnace smoke had abated. It is possible that some wall pipes
were carried up to the height of the eaves and used to discharge smoke into
the open air.

In Italy with its generally mild weather even the richest house would
boast no more than a few favoured rooms heated by the hypocaust method.
Outside the homeland, however, the Romans adapted their building techniques to suit local conditions. Because of the cold, damp climate the
wealthier colonists and romanized nobles of provincial Britain practised a
much fuller form of central heating than was common in metropolitan Italy.
All the major rooms of the great villas which dotted the British countryside
were warmed from under-floor cavities or wall pipes. But such luxury was,
of course, for the civilized minority; the bulk of the British population

continued to live in the traditional round hut heated by a central fire which voided its smoke through a hole in the roof. Ornate andirons, used to prop up burning logs on these simple hearths, were for long considered an essential item in the grave furnishings of a Celtic chieftain.

The Romans were not alone amongst the ancient peoples in their development of under-floor heating. From early times, exactly when is not clear, the Chinese used a method not dissimilar to the hypocaust. Bernan, writing in 1845, described the Chinese system in the following terms. 'At one end of the apartment are massive benches or places, built hollow with bricks, in the form of a bed, which are larger or smaller according to the number of the family. On one side of the bench is a small stove wherein they put charcoal or fossil coal, whose flame and heat are dispersed to all parts, by pipes, which end in a funnel that carries the smoke above the roof.' Unlike the hypocaust whose secret was lost to Rome's barbarian successors, the Chinese bench-stove continued in use down to modern times.

Many skills vanished during the turbulent fifth century when Roman power in Europe collapsed under the successive invasions of the Germanic

The central fire in the fourteenth-century hall of Penshurst Place.

tribes. The Anglo-Saxons who overran much of Britain seem to have had such a mistrust of Roman buildings that they preferred to build afresh. Elegant villas were allowed to fall into decay while Saxon lords erected timber halls with thatched roofs to shelter themselves and their retainers. An earthen floor with a central hob of clay under a smoke-hole in the thatch was the crude Saxon alternative to the Roman heated pavement. The art of domestic heating in the West had received a setback from which it would take 1,400 years to recover.

However, if an open fire was to be used, then the central hearth was not only the simplest way of heating a building, but it also possessed several distinct advantages. Its heat was thrown out evenly in all directions so as to warm the maximum number—an important factor in those days of communal living—while the flames were kept at the greatest possible distance from inflammable timber walls. Natural human conservatism ensured that the central fire continued in vogue long after the rich had begun to build in stone. The beautiful hall of Penshurst Place in Kent, built about 1341, was heated by an open hearth; so was the great hall erected at Eltham Palace as late as about 1480.

With the common people the central fireplace had an even longer life. Chaucer's late fourteenth-century description of a poor widow's home as 'ful sooty' leaves little doubt as to how she heated it, while well over two hundred years later, in about 1610, Bishop Hall could still sneer at a cottage 'whose thatched sparres are furr'd with sluttish soot'. Another writer states explicitly that until the second decade of the seventeenth century some Cheshire farmhouses were heated in 'the old manner of the Saxons'. It seems fairly certain that wall fireplaces and chimneys were almost unknown in the poorer cottages until the middle of the sixteenth century.

The evolution of the wall fireplace and the chimney owed something to the advance of military architecture. In the multi-storey stone castles that the Normans began to build during the eleventh century, chambers on the lower floors could not be heated in the traditional manner because of the difficulty of venting the smoke. Even with the upper rooms there was a snag, since the roof was required as a fighting platform and had to be kept free of obstructing louvers. The Norman masons solved the problem of heating these new-style buildings by moving the fireplace from the centre of the floor to a wall recess. From here angled flues led up through the thickness of the wall to discharge from external smoke holes, one on either side of a buttress. Several fireplaces of this sort are still in existence, the earliest English example, at Colchester Castle in Essex, dating from about 1090. By the middle of the twelfth century vertical flues had come into use

The eleventh-century wall fireplace at Colchester Castle.

The cylindrical stone chimney of a twelfth-century house at Christchurch, Hampshire.

This Dutch interior, painted by Hieronymus Bosch in the fifteenth century, shows the by then old-fashioned hooded fireplace which had been so popular two hundred years before.

During the fifteenth century the pointed Tudor arch was much used for fireplaces. This illustration shows that the design was by no means out of place in an early seventeenth-century setting.

and were sometimes surmounted by cylindrical stone chimneys which carried the smoke to above roof level.

The simple round arch of the first castle fireplaces gradually gave way to more sophisticated designs, some calculated to improve performance but others mere whims of fashion. One useful innovation was the stone hood which projected into the room above the hearth and helped to collect the smoke of the fire. Hooded fireplaces were in use at Conisborough Castle, South Yorkshire, in about 1190. During the succeeding century they gained considerable popularity, before eventually going out of fashion in the early decades of the 1300s.

By this time improvements in chimney construction had made the expensive tapering hood virtually redundant, and it was gradually realized that the simple arched fireplace, which had never been supplanted in the kitchen, could now be used with little fear of its smoking. Before long this cheaper type of fireplace began to creep back into the main hall of even the most aristocratic of buildings, though in keeping with current tastes the old-fashioned rounded opening of the Norman era had been replaced by one of distinctly gothic appearance. During the fifteenth century the pointed Tudor-arch fireplace established itself as the most favoured design.

It was at about this period that supplies of firewood began to run short, 63 so that alternative fuels were needed. In lowland Scotland, which was the first part of the country to feel the pinch, coal was in common use at the close of the fifteenth century. The new fuel demanded a new kind of fireplace. Old-fashioned hearth-stones with andirons against which logs of wood could be piled became out-dated. From the early 1500s Scottish inventories begin to mention 'iron chimleys' or grates adapted to burn coal.

England, with its greater reserves of timber, made little use of coal for domestic fires until the accession of Elizabeth I. From then on the practice of burning coal increased rapidly, so that towards the end of the reign it seemed quite natural for Shakespeare to make his Dame Quickly, in the play *Henry IV, Part 2*, speak of Falstaff enjoying a 'sea cole fire'. A further confirmation of the widespread adoption of the new fuel comes from 1603, the year of the Queen's death, when an inventory was compiled of the goods of Sir Thomas Kytson of Hengrave Hall, Suffolk, in which specific mention

An eighteenth-century hob grate.

was made of a 'cradell of iron for the chimnye to burn secole with'. But the fossil fuel was not without its critics. Ladies believed that its smoke would ruin their complexions, and such was their dread of 'coal tinge' that some even refused to eat food cooked on coal-fired ranges. Perhaps the Virgin Queen had shared her subjects' fears for she had made it illegal for coal to be burnt in London while Parliament was in session. Moryson, writing in 1613 could bemoan the fact that '. . . in some places . . . they burne turffe and the very dung of cowes; yet, in the meantime, England exports great quantities of sea coale to forraine partes'.

The prejudice against coal was to some extent justified. Grates were as yet ill-adapted to its combustion, and consequently generated enormous quantities of sulphurous smoke. City atmospheres suffered from increasing contamination. But fuel of some sort was a necessity, so despite all opposition the trade in coal prospered. London had become so dependent upon it by the Civil War period that great hardship followed the King's seizure of Newcastle in 1644, and his subsequent embargo on coal shipments to his rebellious capital. Jorevin de Rochford, who visited London in about 1670, commented that more of its inhabitants burnt coal than wood. Fireplaces had by this time been improved. Rochford noted that the coal was enclosed in 'a kind of iron cage' and that the nuisance from smoke was less than he had been led to expect.

An early fireplace intended for coal burning is preserved at the London Charterhouse, which was purchased by the coal-merchant, Sir Thomas Sutton, in 1611. Sir Thomas, naturally enough, wanted to warm the dining hall with his own fuel. The new fireplace which he installed had the raised fire-cage needed for coal, but interestingly enough retained the now redundant andirons as a decorative motif.

The next stage in the adaptation of the fireplace to the use of coal was the hob grate, which narrowed down the hearth and provided hotplates on either side of the fire. In its later form, as the elegant duck's-nest grate, this survived into the nineteenth century, but often it suffered from smokiness because the chimney aperture had not been narrowed down from the old wood-burning days. The eighteenth-century Bath fireplace was the west of England's answer to the incorrigible chimney. An iron plate filled the space between the hob grate and the mantel, leaving only a small, arched opening above the fire. This induced an extremely strong air current, which cured the smoking chimney but promoted too rapid a rate of combustion. Bernan, a British heating engineer and historian of heating methods, wrote sarcastically in 1845 that the Bath grate would give 'a roaring fire that will melt gold' and an updraught sufficient to ensure that 'not only the smoke,   65

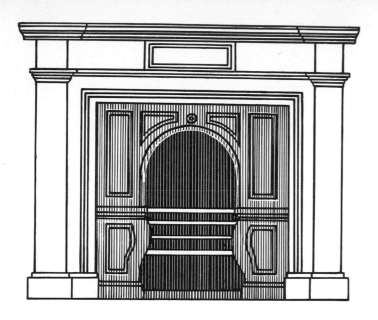

The Bath fireplace gave a roaring fire but consumed prodigious amounts of coal and caused uncomfortable draughts.

but all the air in the room, whisked up the chimney with the velocity of a hurricane, followed by all the comfort at a speed as rapid'.

In his book *Chimney Fireplaces*, published in 1796, Count Rumford showed how a smoking chimney could be rectified without undue waste of fuel. The distance between the top of the fire and the entrance to the flue was the crucial factor. If the gap were too great the hot gases rising from the fire would be over-cooled and the updraught sluggish; if the distance were too small, as in the Bath grate, the hot gases would rush into the flue, wasting heat up the chimney and causing the fire to burn furiously. Rumford found that a distance of 14 to 20 inches (36–51 cm.) between the top of the grate and the flue gave the best results. Another of his useful suggestions was that to improve the flow of chimney gases the entrance to the flue, or throat as he christened it, should be restricted to a depth of 4 inches (10 cm.), although allowed to extend across the width of the fireplace. The grate itself, he advocated, should be brought as far forward as possible while still keeping it directly below the throat of the chimney. Unlike the old-style fireplaces, which had been built as wide at the back as in front, Rumford's were to have their sides splayed to throw as much heat as possible out into the room. Iron-work, he thought, should be kept to the minimum since it conducted heat away and imparted it to the flue gases; instead sides and back were to be made of insulating materials, such as fireclay. Air flow into the base was to be controlled by a tight-fitting fender with adjustable openings. Rumford had come near to inventing the perfect open fire; unfortunately his ideas were only partially accepted, and many nineteenth-century fireplaces ignored most of his carefully worked out principles. Thirty years after the Count's

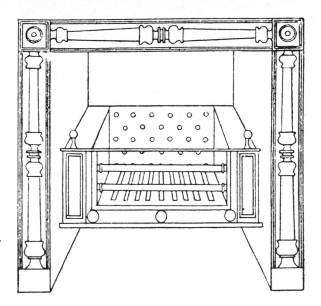

An early nineteenth-century fireplace.

death, Bernan had regretfully to report that although many fireplaces boasted splayed sides and claimed to be 'Rumfordized' 'scarcely one . . . in ten thousand is formed agreeably to his formula'.

Rumford, however, was only one in a long line of fire improvers. While the British had been occupied in learning to cope with coal, others had brought the wood burning grate to a high state of perfection. In his *Architecture Françoise* published in 1624 Louis Savot described an ingenious fireplace which he had seen in the Louvre at Paris. The back, hearth, and sides of this contrivance were made of iron plates fixed to leave a gap of 3 inches (7·6 cm.) between them and the brickwork. Openings at the front of the base plate allowed air to be drawn into the spaces under and around the fire, where it was strongly heated by contact with the hot iron before being

The seventeenth-century fireplace in the Louvre which passed a current of hot air into the room from ducts beneath and behind the open grate.

passed back into the room through channels which emerged just under the mantel shelf. This is the first known attempt at combining the cheerfulness of the open fire with the economy of the closed stove.

The origin of the stove is uncertain. The earliest recorded example in Europe comes from the Alsace region of France in 1490, though the Chinese were probably using similar devices at a much earlier date. But whatever the source of its invention the stove had, by the sixteenth century, found great favour in the colder northern and eastern parts of Europe. Moryson, writing in 1613, praises the economy of the German stove:

> 'The intemperatenesse of colde pressinge great part of Germanie, instead of fier they use hot stoves for remedie thereof, which are certaine chambers of rooms having an earthen oven caste into them, which may be heated with a little quantity of wood, so as it will make them hot who come out of the colde . . .'.

To be at its most effective a stove has to retain the hot combustion gases as long as possible so that they give up most of their heat before escaping into the chimney. In many early European stoves this was achieved by

A model stove in a seventeenth-century German dolls' house.

The cast-iron stove dominated the American interior for much of the nineteenth century. This photograph of a room in a Kansas sod house shows a typical heating arrangement.

passing the smoke from a fire burning in an adjacent room through a large box-like structure which protruded into the chamber to be heated. The eighteenth century produced several refinements in design. So-called Russian stoves, in which the smoke had to make its way through a number of circulating chambers before entering the flue, won wide regard. Swedish stoves also established a high reputation, though with less reason. In these the flue gases were re-heated with the idea of making them burn, but all that was achieved was to send the smoke into the chimney hotter than it need have been.

Stoves never really caught on for domestic heating in Britain, though they secured considerable popularity in the American colonies. Cast-iron stoves were manufactured in Massachusetts from as early as 1642, and by the 1740s the prominent American scientist Benjamin Franklin had established the fundamental principles of stove construction. During the nineteenth century the new republic was manufacturing a bewildering variety of cast-iron stoves, which found their way into every sort of home. Oscar Wilde, who moved in the best of circles, felt compelled to complain on a visit to the United States of the ubiquitous 'heat-radiating decorations in the centre of the room'. In the twentieth century the stove has been toppled from its transatlantic pre-eminence by the widespread adoption of central heating.

69

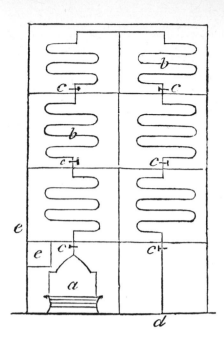

William Cook's scheme for steam heating a house, 1745.

The idea of central heating, which had lain dormant since Roman times, was revived and put to use during the eighteenth century when experiments were carried out with steam, hot-water, and hot-air systems. Public buildings and the developing factories of the Industrial Revolution could not be adequately heated by open fires; nor were stoves really satisfactory. Advancing technology both demanded and was able to supply new forms of heating. Most early central heating systems were installed in factories and hospitals, although a few wealthy and adventurous householders also benefited.

Steam heating was very largely a by-product of the development of the steam engine. Experimenters could hardly fail to notice the great heating power of steam, and, once a manufacturer had installed steam-driven machinery in his factory, it was only a short step to use the same medium for heating.

As long ago as the closing years of the sixteenth century Sir Hugh Platt had outlined a plan for forcing garden plants with steam obtained 'by hanging a cover of tin or other metall over the vessel wherein you boil your beefe or drive your buck', but it was not until 1745 that Colonel William Cook described the first really practicable scheme for steam heating. A steam pipe fed from a central boiler was to be conducted through all the rooms of the house before venting into the open air. The Colonel never put his crude but workable system to the test, and as far as is known the first person actually to heat a room by steam was the famous engineer, James Watt. During the winter of 1784–5 Watt heated his Birmingham work-room with a simple 'radiator', consisting of a shallow box set on edge and fed with steam from a boiler on a lower floor. Although the results of this experiment were below expectations they did not deter Watt's partner, Matthew Boulton, from shortly afterwards using steam to heat a room in his own house. In 1795 he erected a similar apparatus in the library of his friend, Dr. Withering. Experience was accumulating; steam heat was on its way. By 1801 Boulton and Watt had enough confidence to employ an ingenious form of steam heating in the Salford factory which they were constructing for Philips and Lee. The hollow cast-iron pillars which supported the building were made to double as heaters by feeding them with steam from a basement boiler.

Boulton and Watt were not, however, the sole pioneers of steam heat. They made no secret of their experiments, and soon had several competitors. The Halifax inventor, Hoyle, took out a patent for steam heating in 1791 and used his method to heat several cloth factories in his native town, another one at Bradley, and a private house near London. Unfortunately the household apparatus, at least, proved ineffective, and was eventually removed. Neil Snodgrass, who in 1799 used steam to heat a cotton manufactory on the banks of the Spey, was another early heating engineer. Steam heating for factories was well established by 1807, when Buchanan published a pamphlet which for many years remained the most authoritative work on the subject.

Steam was less suited to domestic heating. Pipes got very hot, while water locks caused by condensation could produce the most alarming hammering noises. In Britain, with its temperate climate, steam heating seldom appealed to house owners, but in the colder parts of the United States it did attain some popularity. During the 1880s district heating companies, which piped steam into their customers' homes, came into prominence in many American cities.

Hot-water heating, which finds much more favour in Britain, has a history just as long as that of steam, for it too may be traced back to the writings of that remarkable Elizabethan, Sir Hugh Platt. Sir Hugh was anxious to take the danger out of drying gunpowder and suggested the use of '. . . scalding water at a pipe, which water may be also heated at another room . . .' This idea was revived early in the eighteenth century by a Swedish expatriate, Sir Martin Triewald, who while living in Newcastle-upon-Tyne outlined a scheme for using hot water to heat a greenhouse. It was not, however, until just prior to the French Revolution of 1789 that hot-water heating was put to its first practical use in an incubator designed by M. Bonnemain to hatch chicks for the Paris market. The Marquis de Chabanne adapted Bonnemain's system to domestic heating and introduced it into Britain in 1816. De Chabanne never established a popular reputation, perhaps because he was ahead of his age, but nevertheless his example was important. Bernan, the historian of heating methods, writing in 1845, could confirm that since the Marquis' time 'warming by hot water has been much extended, and some variety introduced into the apparatus'. Robert Briggs began to install hot-water heating systems in the United States during the 1840s. Central heating continued to gain ground during the nineteenth and twentieth centuries, but as late as 1950 the great majority of British houses were still warmed by open fires. Since that date there has been an increasingly rapid swing away from the traditional hearth, the owners of older properties mainly converting to hot-water, the builders of new often preferring ducted warm air.

Modern hot-air heating seems to have been an off-shoot of the common eighteenth-century practice of warming factory buildings with closed stoves. Fire caused by escaping cinders was an ever-present hazard, and to reduce this risk certain owners removed the stove from the shop-floor, locating it instead in a specially built room. Hot air from this stoke-hole was then piped into the main part of the factory. In about 1792 William Strutt improved on this primitive method by confining the furnace inside an arched, brick-built jacket. Cool air was admitted into the 10-inch (25-cm.) gap between the furnace and the jacket walls, and after being strongly heated rose into a pipe for distribution. Joseph Green, another hot-air pioneer, wrongly mistrusted the high temperature of Strutt's furnace and was determined to ensure that the air 'was preserved from being burned, and was always fit for respiration'. In 1793 he took out patents for apparatus intended to heat air by contact with hot water or steam. One of his methods involved passing air through a worm pipe immersed in the hot water of a boiler; another used a small steam pipe to heat air in special ducts provided in each room. Green's latter system failed to give satisfaction in a house on Wimbledon Common, but was more successful in heating a vinery attached to a villa in Hammersmith. The rival schemes adopted so long ago by Strutt and Green still find their counterparts in modern practice. In some cases air is heated directly in a furnace, but in others it is blown through a heat exchanger containing hot water.

Much may be said in favour of ducted warm air, whatever its mode of production. It is both the fastest acting of all central heating systems and the one which makes least demands on the décor of a room. During passage through the ducts the air may be filtered and humidified as well as being heated, while arrangements may also be made to draw in a little fresh air from outside. Since ducts can be installed just as cheaply as hot-water pipes

72

during the construction of a new house, this form of heating is on the increase.

Parallel to the development of central heating came the exploitation of new fuels—gas, electricity, and oil. The first commercial gas company was formed in London in 1812, but it was many years before the public could be persuaded to set aside its not unjustified mistrust of gas as a heating agent. Early experimenters found it difficult to prevent the accumulation of soot and the emission of evil smells. Real success had to wait on a better understanding of combustion and the purification of mains supplies. However, devices like Richard Barnes' convector stove of 1832 and David Owen Edwards' *Atmopyre* of 1849 did serve to encourage further research. The *Atmopyre* is interesting in being the first known attempt to produce a radiant gas fire. It consisted of a hollow clay bulb, from which the gas escaped through many small holes. When a light was applied to the outside the whole surface of the bulb became covered with a 'thin yellow flame'.

After 1850 the number of patents granted for gas fires showed a sharp rise. Several designs appeared which attempted to imitate the cheerful appearance of the open fire, and one devised by George Bower in 1852 may be regarded as a prototype of the modern living-room gas heater. Bower's idea was to build his appliance into an existing fireplace but to replace the usual coal with lumps of asbestos heated by gas flames. Hollow chambers around the

grate were intended to send currents of warm air into the room to supplement the effect of radiation. Smith and Phillips' device of the following year which 'obtained the appearance and effect of an ordinary coal fire by jets of gas radiating upon lumps of glass laid upon a piece of plate glass in the bottom of the stove' acted mainly as a convector heater. This appliance had little to recommend it, since its doubtful visual appeal would have been swiftly obscured by a deposit of soot.

The soot problem was finally solved in 1855 when Robert Wilhelm Bunsen popularized a means of mixing gas with air prior to combustion. Other inventors were not slow to seize their opportunity. Pettit and Smith had a fire on the market in 1856 which used heat 'from gas mixed with atmospheric air before ignition'. From now on advance was rapid, and by the time of the International Electricity and Gas Exhibition held at the Crystal Palace in 1882 it was possible to show a great variety of gas-burning appliances. The typical radiant fire of the period consisted of a firebrick tile, sometimes faced with asbestos, held upright in a cast-iron frame. Flames from a burner in the base impinged on the tile, and brought it to radiant heat. The products of combustion were led into a chimney. Tubular radiants, similar to those in use today, first appeared in 1905.

Four years after Bunsen had put the gas fire firmly on the road to success, the opening up of the Pennsylvanian oil-fields provided the world with yet another fuel. At first the oil was valued mainly for the illuminating power of its kerosene or paraffin fraction, but after the invention of an effective

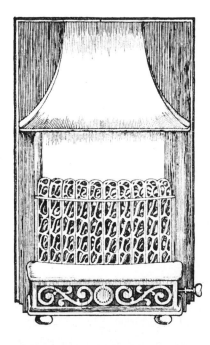

Gas fire, 1927.

Glow-lamp radiator, about 1906.

wick-burner in 1878 the paraffin stove quickly established itself. The practice of using the heavier fractions of oil as a fuel for central heating began on the Pacific coast of the United States and reached significant proportions during the 1920s.

The heating effect of electricity was well known long before Edison established the first public generating station at Pearl Street, New York, in 1881. There were, however, several stumbling blocks in the way of the rapid adoption of electricity for domestic heating. Supplies were limited and costs were high, while there was also a serious technical difficulty in the absence of any wire that could withstand long-term exposure to high temperatures. The disadvantage of high cost has never been completely overcome, which explains the comparative unpopularity of this most flexible of all heating media; answers to the other problem were quickly forthcoming. In 1895, for example, Dowsing cleverly dodged the central issue by suggesting the use of modified incandescent-filament bulbs for heating purposes. The filament, safe within its evacuated envelope, was free from corrosion though very susceptible to mechanical damage. Glow-lamp heaters, as they were called, enjoyed a considerable vogue, and were still in production during the 1920s. Other inventors avoided the difficulty by concentrating on convector heaters in which the electric elements could be run at relatively low temperatures. But a much more fundamental solution was at hand. Early in the present century a nickel-chromium alloy was developed which defied oxidation. The advent of this material marked the beginning of the modern radiant electric fire.

Since the Second World War the long-familiar convectors and radiant fires have experienced competition from newer forms of electrical heating. Storage heaters have appeared to make use of cheaper off-peak electricity,

Belling electric fire, 1915.

Sun-trap panels for solar heating.

while fan heaters, which blow hot air instead of relying on slower natural convection, have come to the fore during the last decade. Underfloor heating is a variation of the storage-heater idea. Heating elements are buried in the concrete ground floor of the house during its construction. A timing mechanism switches on the current at night, so that the block of concrete warms up and stores heat for use next day.

Technology has enabled the householder to cosset himself as never before, but only at the expense of encouraging him to plunder the world's diminishing reserves of fossil fuel. Gas, oil, and coal are burnt in prodigious quantities to provide domestic comfort. Already shortages of natural gas and oil are forecast for the end of the century, so that new methods of house heating must be urgently explored.

Solar heating, which makes no demands on external fuel supplies, provides a promising avenue for research. Unfortunately, although the total sunshine energy reaching the earth is enough to meet humanity's needs 20,000 times over, it is spread so thinly that large catchment areas are needed to collect significant amounts. Another difficulty facing the solar house is that in cold, dull weather the energy supply is reduced just when it is most needed. Nevertheless encouraging results have been achieved, and already many houses in Florida use solar energy to produce domestic hot water. With larger collectors all the heat requirements of these houses could be met for most of the year. Even in the northern state of Massachusetts a solar house

77

was built in 1948 which was able to supply itself with 95 per cent of the heat it needed.

In its usual form the solar-heated house employs flatplate collectors in place of a conventional roof. Each collector consists of a sandwich of plate-glass cover, air-gap filling, and blackened sheet-metal bottom. Water or air circulated through ducts attached to the metal sheets draws off the accumulated heat for storage against future needs. It is with storage, however, that the main snag is encountered. To heat a mere two rooms at the moment requires a 1,200-gallon tank of water. Practical difficulties abound, but there can be little doubt that once conventional fuels run short solar energy will make a major contribution to continuing domestic comfort.

Britain with its cloudy climate will probably seek other solutions. Nuclear energy may replace coal and oil for the generation of electricity; huge satellites may beam down solar energy to waiting cities; the interior heat of the earth itself may be tapped. Change is inevitable, but one thing remains certain. A world-wide civilization cannot be maintained without the help of domestic heating.

4

A Light in the Window

Early man spent much of his waking life in search of food. Home was merely the place to which he returned to sleep, and it mattered little if such a shelter were dark so long as it was weatherproof. Illumination was more accidental than intentional. During the day sunshine filtered in through the entrance, while at night a never-dying fire combined a friendly glow with a comforting warmth.

Doors must have doubled for windows long after man moved out of the caves and primitive pit dwellings of his infancy. In tropical countries the strength of the sunlight made windows less desirable, and to this day many traditional houses in Africa are devoid of any openings other than their doors. The origin of windows must probably be sought in cooler, dimmer regions. House models made in central Europe during the fourth millennium B.C., if not earlier, sometimes have their walls pierced by circular holes which are strongly suggestive of windows. But it is only with the development in ancient Egypt and Iraq of the world's first great civilizations that the existence of the window becomes a certainty. Wall paintings, models, and actual buildings all provide undeniable evidence, and from this time onwards the window has a continuous history.

The Sumerians of Iraq favoured the courtyard house, which turned its back on the sun and looked inwards on itself. Most rooms communicated directly with the shaded court through open doors, so that windows in the outer wall could be limited to tiny openings covered by grilles of clay or wood. Archaeologists have uncovered Sumerian window grilles of the third millennium B.C.

In Egypt, too, the fierce climate made the courtyard house popular, but often were rooms arranged along only two sides of the court, which was enclosed on its other flanks by plain mud-brick walls. External windows were small or sometimes omitted altogether, since rooms bordering the courtyard were frequently left open on that side. The small Egyptian house looked like a miniature fortress. Larger houses would have had more need

A Sumerian window grille of the
third millennium B.C.

for windows, and a mural painting from as early as the middle of the third
millennium B.C. shows a mansion in which the several wall openings were
provided with matting screens to cut down the glare of the midday sun.
Already the window was progressing beyond the stage of a mere gap in
the wall.

During the second millennium B.C. the Minoans of island Crete developed
the window still further. They felt no desire to hide from the sun, and their
multi-storey houses gazed out on the world through wide openings, intended
to let in a flood of light. Some Minoan windows were, in fact, so large that
they could not be left as plain holes in the wall without considerably weaken-
ing the house structure. The Minoan builders solved this problem by
using, and possibly inventing, the vertical mullion and the horizontal
transom, which reinforced the window by dividing it into four sections.

The next major advance in window design did not occur until early in
the Christian era, when the Romans began to make a limited use of glass
and mica panes. In Britain fragments of translucent, greenish-blue glass
are found on the sites of Roman villas, but it is not known how widely
glazed windows were employed in the warmer parts of the empire. Probably
glass was installed only by the richer households, since expensive bronze
frames were needed to support the small, thick panes, which were all that
contemporary technology could supply. No trace of glass or mica has been
found in association with the ruined insulae of Ostia, so it seems unlikely
that either they or the tenements of nearby Rome were ever blessed with
the luxury of glazed windows. Ordinary Romans could keep out the wind

or the rain only by closing their wooden shutters and excluding the daylight as well.

The whole quality of European life deteriorated when the barbarians overran the Western Roman Empire during the fifth century. Violence became rife, and as society crumbled many of the skills developed under the long Roman peace were lost. The domestic glass window was one of the casualties of the great upheaval. Many centuries were to pass before even the kings of the new nations that slowly emerged out of the ruins of the classical world learnt to value the comfort of adequate glazing. Panes of ground-down horn were occasionally used in the private rooms of aristocratic households, but much more frequently noblemen and retainers alike shivered in the draught from open windows. For both security and warmth wall openings had to be small, no matter how important the house, and in the poor man's cottage windows were often omitted altogether. But for the

An open Norman window.

Church's recognition of the dignity imparted to a building by the use of glass, the art of glazing might easily have died out as completely on the Continent as it did in Saxon England. English records of the seventh century reveal that, in the absence of any native glaziers, craftsmen had to be recruited in Gaul to provide windows for the monasteries at Monkwearmouth and Jarrow.

Secular glass windows remained extremely rare in the West until the thirteenth century, despite the ecclesiastical example. The feudal lords of earlier years were of a hardy breed which would rather spare its purse than its person. While the price of glass continued high, the windows of Europe's mighty stone castles stood open to the elements during the day and were closed by wooden shutters during the night. Gradually, however, a taste for new luxuries began to grow. Crusaders, who came into contact with a Byzantine culture that still practised the Roman arts of glazing and central heating, were made sharply aware of the inadequacies of domestic arrangements at home. Increasingly the windows of the solar, the lord's private bed-sitting-room, were screened with one material or another. Sometimes a piece of greased cloth served to keep out the wind and let in the light, but diamond-shaped panes of horn set in lead were also used. Once this concession to luxury became firmly established, it was only a matter of time before glass replaced its makeshift substitutes. All that was needed was a reduction in cost.

At first only the mightiest—king, nobles, and wealthy merchants—could afford the benefits of glass. Henry III was the first English monarch to use the material on a large scale. Prior to his reign (1216–72) even the windows of the royal palaces seem to have been unglazed. His records are full of references to new glass windows. At Winchester workmen were ordered to install 'two glass windows to shut and open, in our chamber, opposite our bed', while at Clipstone instructions were given for the privies used by the king and queen to be glazed. Similar improvements went forward at other royal residences, and courtiers were no doubt quick to imitate their master. The hinged glass window, which could be left open in fine weather and closed without obliterating the light in bad, was too great an advance to be spurned once it had been experienced.

As political stability improved in the later Middle Ages, the need for defensive building was reduced, and the houses of the aristocracy began to relax their fortress-like appearance. Window sizes increased, but it long remained a common practice for lower portions to be shuttered and for only the upper parts to be glazed. Glass continued so expensive that until the sixteenth century casements were often taken down and stored away

A fourteenth-century window in the manor-house at Meare, Somerset.

during a prolonged absence from home. According to an account of 1584 the country people of the previous generation had used 'much latisse and that made either of wicker or fine rifts of oake in chekerwise'. It was not until the late eighteenth century that a writer could claim: 'Glass is at length introduced into windows of most cottages.'

During the 500 years that elapsed between the re-introduction of domestic glass in western Europe and its almost universal adoption, there were many innovations and changes in fashion in window design. Round-headed and pointed openings were gradually superseded by rectangular windows, while increasingly stone tracery was replaced by wooden mullions and transoms.

Fifteenth-century windows are shown in this old engraving of a house in Bristol.

Bay windows first became fashionable in the fourteenth century and have retained their popularity ever since. The example shown comes from Cowdray, which was built in about 1530.

A mid-seventeenth century window showing the typical small leaded lights.

From the end of the seventeenth century the sliding sash window came into vogue temporarily eclipsing the hinged casement. Projecting windows were another development. The men of the fourteenth century appreciated the pleasure to be had from sitting in a glass-enclosed alcove, and began to push out ground-floor windows to form bays. Oriels or upper-floor bays originated earlier still, becoming fashionable during the reign of Henry III.

Glazing methods, however, were slower to alter. It was not until late in the seventeeth century that large glass panes held by wooden glazing bars began to take over from the old-fashioned leaded lights. This new departure coupled with improvements in glass technology enabled a progressive increase in the size of window panes. By Victorian times such large sheets of glass could be manufactured that glazing bars were often omitted altogether.

While glass eventually became an indispensable part of the European home, some of the peoples of the Far East brought the use of alternative materials to a fine art. The windows of traditional houses in Japan and China are divided into many sections to support such delicate coverings as translucent shell, cloth, or frequently oiled paper. Such windows are far from primitive. They slide neatly sideways to provide extra light and ventilation, and their lattice-work conforms to well-defined conventions. Glass windows are, however, gaining ground, as more and more oriental town dwellers move into western-style apartment blocks. Regrettably regional differences are fast disappearing in this world of instant communication.

Man's conquest of distance extends also to a new mastery of materials. The international architecture of steel frame and reinforced concrete frees large areas of wall from load bearing duties. Apartment-block windows

Georgian windows with large panes and narrow wooden glazing bars, Bedford Square, London.

Traditional Japanese windows.

may be made just as large or small as the designer wishes. Sound and heat insulation are improved by double glazing, while windows have even been devised which allow people to look out but not in. The window has come a long way since it started as a mere hole in the wall some 6,000 years ago.

Artificial lighting is older than any window. It began at least 360,000 years ago when primitive man-like creatures, living in what is now China, learnt to use and control fire. Initially, the flames were valued much more for their heat than their light, but as man developed he became less prepared to spend all the hours of darkness in sleep. Little portable fires were devised to give a comforting circle of light and drive back the frightening shadows of the night.

Wooden torches were probably the first step away from dependence on fire-light, but lamps are very old. The hundred or so left behind by the artists, who decorated the Lascaux Caves in France with magical hunting scenes 15,000 years ago, have a refinement of design which suggests a long history. Each was made from a well-shaped piece of sandstone with a shallow bowl scooped out to hold animal fat. Moss was quite possibly used to form a wick. Similar stone lamps found in Czechoslovakia are thought to be almost twice as ancient.

Gradually design was improved. A groove was cut to carry the wick to the edge of the lamp so that some downward illumination became possible,

Stone Age lamp.

while additional wicks were used to give more light. New materials took over from stone. Terracotta lamps dating from about 8000 B.C. have been found in Iraq. But basically the method of lighting remained unchanged. The flickering oil-fed flames which lit the houses and palaces of Sumer and Egypt during the third millennium B.C. would have caused little surprise to the Lascaux cave-artists.

At the time when the Sumerians of Iraq were establishing their cities along the Tigris and Euphrates, the waters of the Persian Gulf stretched much farther inland than they do today. Large seashells were easily obtainable, and it seems to have long been the custom to use them as lamps. Examples from Ur show how the natural openings were enlarged for ease of filling, while the lip of the shell was utilized as a channel for the wick. Tradition was so strong that even the stone or metal lamps made for the wealthy conformed to some extent to the shape of a shell. The type of fuel burnt in Sumerian lamps is still a matter of dispute. Vegetable oil was extracted from the sesame seed, but some authorities maintain that crude mineral oil was preferred for lighting purposes. This belief is given some weight by the certain fact that the Sumerians made torches, as a cheap alternative to lamps, by dipping bundles of reeds in surface out-wellings of oil.

Surprisingly little is known about the methods the Egyptians used to light their homes. Positively identified lamps are rare, although the Louvre Museum in Paris does possess a copper dish of third or fourth dynasty origin (about 2700 B.C.) with a lip bent out to receive a wick. This, however, was probably an unusual form, since the Egyptian lamps described by the Greek traveller, Herodotus, in the fifth century B.C. were simple saucer-like bowls with wicks floating in a mixture of castor oil and salt. Many ancient

88

Lamp from ancient Egypt.

pottery vessels of unknown function may, in fact, be lamps. Finds in the tomb of the Pharaoh Tutankhamen, who died in about 1350 B.C., show that the lamp was not disdained by the mighty. What were at first thought to be alabaster vases turned out to be lamp-holders, which, when illuminated from within, revealed previously invisible coloured decorations. The secret was that each holder was made in two pieces, with a blank exterior hiding the painted inner vessel. The Egyptians also possessed wax torches, some of which were found amongst Tutankhamen's treasure, but probably these were used for ceremonial purposes only.

Although the Indus Valley civilization was later and shorter-lived than that of either Egypt or Sumer, it produced a standard of living for its ordinary people unsurpassed by the older cultures. Indus towns like Mohenjo-daro and Harappā, which flourished from about 2300 to 1750 B.C., could boast adequate numbers of communal wells, effective drainage, and many substantial houses. The same careful thought was shown when it came to lighting. Pottery hanging lamps have been found, but the fixed installations were far more ingenious. House walls were built with occasional projecting bricks, each scooped out to hold a supply of oil for a wick.

Centuries passed but still the lamp remained man's most effective source of artificial light. It was used by the Chinese from at least 1600 B.C., and was commonplace throughout the ancient Middle East. Extremely refined varieties were devised. By half-way through the second millennium B.C. the citizens of Troy in northwestern Turkey had perfected a lamp which pre-heated its own oil, while their contemporaries, the Canaanites of Palestine, had produced a seven-wick light for use in temples. It was probably lamps of this multi-wick type that inspired the Israelites to make what the Bible misleadingly called a 'seven-branched candlestick'.

89

The demand for light increased as civilization prospered. Lamps were used in such numbers in classical Greece that thousands have been unearthed in Athens alone. But it was the Romans who brought the production of lamps to its peak. Factories were set up all over the empire, and even the barbarous province of Britain boasted several. Nearly everyone could afford a pottery lamp, though canny peasants still often preferred the expedient of an oil-filled snail shell imbedded in a lump of clay. Wealthy homes were prodigal in their use of light. Metal candelabra from which clusters of multi-wick lamps could be hung still survive, while individual lamps with as many as fourteen burners have been found.

Despite its popularity and widespread use, the oil-filled lamp was not Rome's only source of artificial light. Candles were also burnt from at least the first century B.C. onwards. The early history of the candle has not yet been unravelled. It is just possible that some of the Egyptian wax torches contained wicks, while a fifth century B.C. stand of Etruscan origin has been tentatively identified as a socket candlestick. Definite evidence for the existence of the candle is, however, lacking before the Roman writer Varro (116–27 B.C.) described the 'candela' as a burning rope. Pliny the Younger (A.D. 62–about 114) went further and noted down an account of its manufacture. It is not known how widely the candle was used in the ancient world, but a fair number of candlesticks have been recovered. Most of these were of the socket variety, which suggests that candles were mass produced to a standard size.

With the fall of Rome, European civilization faltered and almost came to an end. The fabric of society collapsed, travel became dangerous, and trading was drastically reduced. Large-scale production could not be maintained, and many industrial arts were lost. When lamps were broken,

Greek lamp of the classical period.

Roman lamps.

they could not be replaced; when oil stocks became depleted, they were difficult to replenish. Most Europeans were reduced to a reliance on man's first means of artificial lighting—the domestic hearth.

But in the Eastern Roman Empire, based on the great city of Constantinople, things went on much as they had done for centuries. Lamps and candles allowed social life to continue long into the night, and city thoroughfares were so busy after dark that street lighting became a necessity. Special taxes to pay for street lamps were levied by the Emperor Justinian, who reigned from A.D. 527–565.

Although the Byzantines adopted the western candle, they looked to Egypt for their lamps. The typical Roman lamp had resembled a diminutive flattened teapot, with a central hole for filling and a spout for the wick. The Byzantine lamp, from the fourth century A.D. onwards, was commonly an open vessel, often made of glass, with a floating-wick such as the Egyptians had used from time immemorial. A few open-bowl lamps, possibly derived from Eastern examples, were even used in 'Dark Age' Europe. Some of the glass jars found in the rich Anglo-Saxon cemetery at Faversham in Kent make more sense as lights than as drinking cups, while there can be no doubt that the saucer-shaped object recovered from a Viking ship burial in Norway was in fact a lamp.

Lamps, however, must have continued a rare luxury in northern Europe until grease burning varieties were developed or easier access to the vegetable oils of the warmer south was re-established. In France, with its Mediterranean contacts, lamps may have come back into fairly general use from as early as the ninth century, but in most lands timber for long remained the   91 chief illuminant. The barn-like dwelling of the Saxon noble was lit by a great wood fire and torches of natural pitch pine or fat-soaked wood flaring from holders ranged along the walls. Candles, despite their uninterrupted use in churches, do not seem to have been re-adopted for domestic lighting until the twelfth century.

The eleventh and twelfth centuries marked a quickening in the tempo of European life. Trade increased, and towns began to prosper and grow. Slowly, very slowly as the standard of housing improved, a demand for better lighting made itself felt. Curfew regulations, aimed at reducing the risk of fire, were relaxed, so that householders were no longer expected to douse all flames as soon as the warning bell had rung. The general ban on any form of domestic lighting after curfew hours, which had oppressed England since the time of the Norman conquest, was lifted by the third Norman king, Henry I, in 1100. Life was being rescued from a monotonous round of work and sleep. By the thirteenth century it was possible, in the words of an anonymous writer, to enjoy 'al longe nigt songs and candle light'.

Two types of candle were known in the Middle Ages—a cheaper kind, made out of tallow, and a more expensive beeswax variety. Of these the tallow candle enjoyed far wider currency, for although wax carried more prestige its cost put it out of the reach of all except the church and the higher nobility. Many households made their own tallow candles, but in town professional chandlers began to tour the streets, touting for business. Such craftsmen would take the customer's own raw materials and turn them into expertly made candles. By 1260 there were enough tallow chandlers in Paris for them to form a trade guild of their own, with nearly a hundred members. Candle-light had become popular with those who could afford it.

Before moulds were introduced, probably in the fourteenth century, tallow candles were made by repeated dipping, while at least until the eighteenth century wax candles were manufactured by pouring and rolling. Such methods did not lend themselves to a uniformity of product; no batch was exactly the same as its predecessor. Socket holders were therefore impracticable, and pricket candlesticks found much more favour, since they could be used with candles of any size. Neither wax nor tallow is hard, so there was little problem in pushing the candle on to its spike. Of the many holders which have survived from the Middle Ages most are of the pricket sort. These ranged from single candlesticks to many-branched candelabra. There were also circular coronae and chandeliers, which were

suspended from the ceiling.

A fourteenth-century miniature showing the floor-standard type of candlestick used by wealthy households.

But even tallow candles were a rich man's light except in the sheep rearing areas of England where the annual autumn killing made meat cheap and mutton grease a commonplace. In these fortunate regions cottage wives saved the fat from their cooking, and made a supply of rush-wicked candles to last them through the dark winter months. Away from the sheep-folds, however, meat was rarely eaten, so that peasants had to eke out their meagre stores of fat. Instead of building up thick candles by several successive dippings, they contented themselves with giving the rushes they had collected a thin coating of grease. The resulting rushlights had to be burnt at an angle, and consequently scattered the floor with droplets of melted fat, but a two foot length could give a reasonable light for half-an-hour. Rushlights were so cheap and economical that they were made and used in the remoter country districts of England down to the early years of Victoria's reign. Even at that late date simple split-stick supports were not unknown in the poorer cottages, although metal holders had been introduced as long ago as the fifteenth century.

Throughout the medieval period and, indeed, well into modern times, the form of lighting adopted by country people was strongly influenced by local conditions and customs. Money was short and transportation difficult.   93

Cottagers had to make do with those materials they could find close at hand. In England it was the rush, but in Scandinavia it was the resinous wood of the pine. A sixteenth-century Swedish writer, Olaus Magnus, noted that the inhabitants of the far north made 'candles of pine, finely split' which 'are sometimes as long as their arms, according to the length of the night'. Across the Baltic Sea in Latvia this practice was still going strong at the end of the nineteenth century. An account published in Russia in 1907 tells how the old Lettish farmers had, within living memory, manufactured splints by splitting them from birch logs dried behind the oven. Splints were also much used in parts of Scotland and Ireland.

The same solution to the problem of lighting had occurred to certain tribes of North American Indians. Early settlers, cut off as they were from supplies of conventional candles, took up the idea out of necessity. Pitch pine candles remained a common illuminant in New England for many years. The Reverend Higginson of Salem enthused in 1630 that the slivers of pine were 'so full of turpentine that they burn as clear as a torch'. Winter, writing in 1642, had reservations. He allowed that candlewood might be useful to poorer people, but went on: '. . . I cannot commend it for a singular good because it droppeth a pitch form of substance where it stands.'

Peasants in southern Europe did not have to contend with messy splints of woods. Vegetable oil was cheap, and snail shells easily found. Improvised lamps, such as had been used since Roman times, could be found in Italy until near the present day.

As the Middle Ages progressed lamps also began to find a wider application in the colder parts of Europe. The classical lamp had disappeared

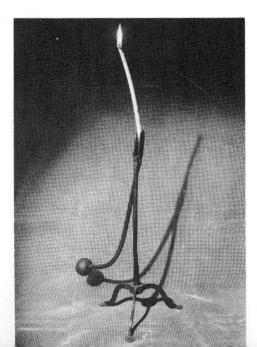

Rushlight holder.

with the supplies of Mediterranean olive oil, but new varieties had been developed to take its place. All were open, and many seem to have been intended to burn tallow. Typical was the cresset stone, much used in English churches and monasteries until at least the end of the medieval period. In its simplest form this was merely a lump of rock hollowed out to make a reservoir for the fuel. Many cresset stones, however, were multiple. The monks at Durham had two twelve-holed cressets to light their dormitory, according to a sixteenth-century inventory, while a surviving stone from Brecon contains thirty depressions. Smaller grease-fed lights must have been used in the domestic setting, and ordinary pottery bowls or saucers were probably pressed into service as float-wick lamps.

For centuries there was no fundamental progress in methods of illumination. Socket candlesticks began to take over from prickets after about 1500, while crystal chandeliers appeared a little later, but these were mere changes in fashion. Except perhaps in quantity, eighteenth-century domestic lighting showed little improvement over that of the fifteenth. The wealthy still used wax candles; the middle classes tallow except on special occasions; the poor whatever local materials their forefathers had learnt to employ. Prodigality with light remained rare. Quite well-to-do people commonly made shift with two candles to a room. It was only in the most fashionable houses that the great two- or three-tiered candelabra and multi-armed wall sconces could be found. This was partly because of the cost of candles, and partly because of the army of servants needed to trim the wicks.

It was not until the last quarter of the eighteenth century that a real break-through in illumination was achieved by the Swiss scientist, Ami Argand. In a series of experiments, beginning in 1782, Argand attempted to increase the light output of the oil lamp by improving the air supply to its wick. A year later he was able to exhibit a lamp to members of the French Academy of Sciences, who reported somewhat optimistically that it gave 'as much light as twenty tallow candles'. The secret lay in the shape of the wick, which was curled round to form a tube, so funnelling air into the centre of the flame. A glass chimney above the wick encouraged an even stronger draught. These two devices promoted such vigorous burning that a light of unparalleled brilliance was emitted. By 1784 the new lamp was on the market in England, and by 1785 a pirated version, manufactured by Quinquet, was being sold in France. The Argand lamp quickly established itself as a favourite amongst the wealthy, though its high purchase price put it out of reach of the majority. Many famous people lit their homes with Argands. In America three lamps of this type are numbered amongst the belongings of George Washington, while in Britain the City of London presented the victorious Duke of Wellington with two massive Argand candelabra. The oldest known existing Argand is an English model of 1784, imported into the United States by Thomas Jefferson, author of the Declaration of Independence.

But no sooner had the oil lamp reached this new perfection than a challenger, in the form of coal-gas, appeared on the horizon. The key figure in the early history of gas was the Scottish engineer William Murdoch, who in 1792 succeeded in lighting his office at Redruth, Cornwall, by burning a vapour distilled from coal. In the early nineteenth century Murdoch's idea was taken up with great enthusiasm by German-born Frederick Albert Winser, whose public lectures did much to promote the formation of the London-based Gas Light and Coke Company in 1812. However, there was a considerable prejudice against gas, and the company was unable to pay a dividend until 1817. Even then gas was for long used to light only streets, factories, and public buildings. Its impact on domestic lighting was extremely limited before the 1840s.

While gas was still struggling to make its way, the competitive position of the common candle as a source of light was considerably strengthened by a number of innovations. First, in 1820, Cambacères found that if a wick were made by plaiting strands of cotton rather than merely twisting them, its end would curl outwards to the hot exterior of the flame and be burnt away. Time-consuming trimming or snuffing of the wick was no longer

William Murdoch's office at Redruth, Cornwall, lit by gas lights, 1792.

Victorian paraffin lamp with a twin-wick duplex burner.

needed to prevent the candle losing its efficiency. In addition advances in chemical science during the 1820s provided candle manufacturers with a new substance, stearin, which burnt with a clear, clean flame. By 1840 the British firm of Price's was able to retail its 'snuffless composite candles' at the remarkably low cost of a shilling a pound. The opening up of the Pennsylvania oil-field in the 1860s made available a new and even cheaper candle material, paraffin wax, but it also brought large quantities of mineral oil on to the market. The abundance of this low-priced fuel caused a revival of interest in the oil lamp.

Kerosene or paraffin was the lamp-maker's dream come true. It was fairly inert, not too smelly, gave a good, smoke-free flame, and above all was cheaper than any other oil. An ordinary flat wick could draw up enough paraffin to supply the flame without resorting to gravity feed or a pumping mechanism. The success of the paraffin lamp was completely assured when, in 1865, the Englishman Hinks introduced the twin-wick duplex burner, which could give out a really powerful light. But for the accidents caused by dropping lamps, the advent of cheap paraffin would have presented a serious   97 threat to the spread of gas-lighting to further city homes. As it was paraffin remained in use in the country long after gas had been replaced by electricity in town.

As long ago as 1802 Sir Humphry Davy had used a current of electricity to heat strips of platinum to incandescence. Electric lighting had been proved feasible, but there were many obstacles to be surmounted before it could become a commercial proposition. The prime requirement was for a reliable source of electricity other than the prohibitively expensive battery. Without ready access to power even the most perfect electric light would be useless. This stumbling block was removed in 1870, when the Belgian engineer, Théophile Gramme, invented the predecessor of the modern dynamo, but other problems had yet to be solved. How could a filament be kept white-hot without excessive heat losses? How could a material be made incandescent without burning away? The answer to both these difficulties seemed to lie in surrounding the filament with a vacuum, but until 1875 no pump existed that could remove quite enough air. It was Sir William Crookes' improvements to the earlier Sprengel pump which opened the way for Swan and Edison's incandescent filament lamps.

Englishman Joseph W. Swan had been working on carbon filament electric lights since 1848, but had continually been baulked by his inability to produce a high enough vacuum. Now he seized his chance, and in 1878 was able to exhibit a reasonably long-lasting lamp, consisting of a carbon filament mounted in an evacuated glass vessel. The filament, which was made by treating a thread of cotton with sulphuric acid, was, however, very fragile.

A much later starter was the American inventor Thomas A. Edison, who, working completely independently, produced his own type of electric lamp in 1879, after a whirlwind of research lasting only eighteen months. In 1880 Edison devised a slightly more robust lamp utilizing a carbonized bamboo filament, but two years later Swan went one better and invented the still stronger squirted nitro-cellulose filament. At this point the two men, who had been squabbling over precedence, became reconciled, and in 1883 combined to form the Edison and Swan United Electric Light Co. Ltd. Electric lighting was now a force to be reckoned with, but gas still had a few tricks up its sleeve.

An extremely hot, though non-luminous gas flame had been available since the German chemist Robert Wilhelm Bunsen invented his burner in 1855. Now minds began to search for a means of turning this heat into a light strong enough to compete with the electric lamp. It was the Austrian, Carl Auer von Welsbach, who found the answer. The first clue came in

Edison electric lights in the drawing-room of a New York house, 1881.

1885 when he discovered that the oxides of certain rare elements became incandescent in the Bunsen flame. After several more years of patient development, he perfected a technique by which a small sleeve of cotton fabric was first impregnated with chemicals and then treated to leave behind only a fine network of thorium and cerium oxides. The Welsbach incandescent mantle was marketed on a large scale from 1893, and kept gas in the forefront of domestic lighting until electric power became much more readily available during the second decade of the twentieth century.

Meanwhile the electric light bulb was being improved by the introduction of new filament materials. Most satisfactory was the high melting point metal, tungsten, which William D. Coolidge learnt to draw into wires in 1909. The filament was now much less susceptible to mechanical damage, but a new difficulty arose. Evaporating metal blackened the inside of evacuated bulbs, making them grow dimmer as they aged. This could be cured by filling with an inert gas, but only at the expense of losing a lot of heat energy by convection. Irving Langmuir came up with a solution to this problem in 1913. By winding the filament of his argon-filled lamp into a tight spiral he cut down the excessive loss of heat, and gave a brighter light for the same consumption of electricity. In 1934 light output was further enhanced by coiling the coiled filament on itself. The incandescent electric lamp had achieved its modern form, and was now ten times more efficient than the early bulbs of Edison and Swan.

Heating to incandescence is, however, a comparatively crude method of illumination, since it inevitably entails the waste of energy in the form of heat. It is far more efficient to produce light by an electrical discharge through a gas. Mercury vapour lamps were used for industrial purposes in the United States from 1903, but the strong blue-green light emitted made them unsuited to the home. The modern fluorescent tubular lamp was a product of the 1930s. Ultra-violet radiation generated by the passage of a current of electricity through the tube stimulated an internal coating of phosphorescent material, which then gave out a well-balanced light. Fluorescent tubes came on to the market in the United States in 1938, and were rapidly accepted for factory, shop, and office lighting. It took much longer for them to make any impact on the domestic scene, but gradually more and more families have come to recognize their advantages. They are cheap to run, free from glare, and throw no sharp shadows. Kitchens and other working rooms may be brilliantly lit, while in living areas cool-running tubes may be hidden away to give soft, concealed lighting. After 360,000 years man has finally liberated himself from reliance on flame, and can now light his house with the flick of a switch.

5

Water

No home can exist without access to water, so until mankind learnt to transport it over long distances, settlements had inevitably to cluster around rivers, springs, or lakes. House sites were chosen to ensure that nature delivered an unfailing supply to the doorstep, but means had to be found to bring the water inside. Containers had to be improvised, large enough to make the journey to the water's edge worthwhile. The form of such vessels depended on local conditions. In pre-pottery Europe water was probably fetched from streams in rush-woven baskets lined with clay. Africa, more blessed with resources, possessed several ready-made containers. The hard shell of the gourd was widely used as a bottle, while up to comparatively recent times the ostrich egg found favour with certain tribes.

The first large-scale efforts to improve on natural water supplies began amongst the farming communities of Mesopotamia in about 4000 B.C. Villagers got together and dug irrigation ditches to bring life-giving water to fields remote from the rivers. As the network of waterways gradually expanded and more and more land was brought under cultivation, farming villages blossomed into towns. These new urban centres were more secure from attack and provided an environment in which specialized trades could flourish, but their very size brought problems. The heavy concentration of population caused river pollution on an unprecedented scale, while many of the new townspeople found that the daily chore of drawing water now involved a tiresomely long journey. Most citizens seem to have resigned themselves to these disadvantages, but a few were rich or energetic enough to procure a local and unpolluted supply of water by digging a private well. A rare third millennium B.C. example has been found at the city of Eshnunna, twenty-five miles northeast of modern Baghdad.

Water was not used merely for drinking and agricultural purposes. The nobility of Mesopotamia developed a high regard for cleanliness, and recognizable bathrooms have been discovered in several ruined palaces

A well-head from the Indus city of Mohenjo-daro.

of the late third millennium. The palace of Eshnunna, for example, boasted not one but five bathrooms, each draining into the large main sewer. Lesser Mesopotamians probably did not share their rulers' enthusiasm for total immersion. Perhaps they occasionally went down to the river to bathe, but within their own homes their habits were simpler. In the middle-class houses of about 1800 B.C., excavated at the city of Ur, the floor of the entrance lobby was usually provided with a drain, so that people who came in from the street could pour water over their feet and hands to wash away the dust.

Like their Mesopotamian contemporaries the ancient Egyptians relied very largely on river water to supply domestic needs. Water for cooking and drinking was carried up to the houses just as in Mesopotamia, but when it came to washing it seems that the Egyptians often reversed the process and took themselves to the water. In the Bible the Book of Exodus tells how the thirteenth-century B.C. prophet Moses was found, as a baby, when 'the daughter of Pharaoh came down to wash herself at the river'. Later in the same Book Moses receives the command of the Lord to:

'Get thee unto Pharaoh in the morning: lo, he goeth out unto the water; and thou shalt stand by the river's brink against he come.'

Evidently the ruler of all Egypt did not think it beneath his dignity to take a bath in the Nile.

Arrangements were far more refined in the cities which flourished along the Indus Valley from about 2300 to 1700 B.C. These cities made elaborate provision not only for the supply and use of water, but also for its final disposal. Each housing block had at least one well of its own so that water could be had without the need for a long trudge down to the river. Perhaps it was because of this comparatively easy availability that bathrooms came to be built in many quite modest homes. Waste water was discharged into a network of open, brick-lined street-drains.

In Mesopotamia and the Indus Valley the bath had been no more than a depression in the floor of a suitably waterproofed room. It took the sparkling genius of Minoan Crete to invent the free-standing tub. Several baths of amazingly modern appearance have been unearthed on the island. One, which comes from the queen's bathroom in the palace of Knossos itself, has a good claim to be the most ancient bath-tub in existence. The room was originally set up in about 1650 B.C., and although the bath is probably a replacement, it must be at least 3,500 years old.

The Cretans built short conduits to bring water from local springs into their palaces and public buildings, but such small-scale works hardly deserve to be called aqueducts. Even if early irrigation ditches are excluded, and only schemes intended to supply at least some domestic water considered, the first real aqueducts still seem to have originated in the Middle East. Sennacherib, King of Assyria from 704 to 681 B.C., built a 30-mile (48-km.) canal with the twin function of supplying water to his palace and irrigating the parks and orchards which he had planted around his capital of Nineveh. The canal itself was a considerable engineering achievement,

Reconstruction of the Queen's bathroom in the palace of Knossos.

but even more impressive was the 300-yard (270-m.) long bridge that carried the waterway over an intervening valley. This multi-arched structure, rising to a height of 25 feet (7·6 m.), was probably the first raised aqueduct of the type later made famous by the Romans.

A contemporary of Sennacherib, Hezekiah, King of Judah from 728 to 697 B.C., constructed an aqueduct with a very different form and function. When the Assyrians threatened to invade his country and lay siege to his cities Hezekiah secured a water supply for all the citizens of Jerusalem by digging a tunnel 1,776 feet (540 m.) long to carry the waters of an external spring to an underground pool within the walls. This act of forethought is justly celebrated in the Bible (2 Kings XX. 20).

> 'And the rest of the acts of Hezekiah, and all his might, and how he made a pool, and a conduit, and brought water into the city, are they not written in the book of the chronicles of the kings of Judah?'

In ancient Greece the rival city states were so often at war that they too could not afford to expose their water supplies to enemy action. Wherever possible they relied on springs, wells, and rainwater cisterns within their walls, and it was only when these sources were completely outgrown that they reluctantly contemplated the construction of aqueducts. If an aqueduct had to be built, its conduit was buried underground to keep it out of sight of marauding soldiers.

One of the earliest Greek aqueducts was constructed during the latter part of the sixth century B.C. to supply the city of Vathy on the island of Samos. A 900-foot (270-m.) hill stood between the town and the chosen spring, so that a tunnel had to be driven for almost a mile through solid rock before the waters could be tapped. Earthenware pipes were used to distribute the clear spring water that issued from the tunnel to the various public fountains of the city. Athens was also provided with an underground aqueduct to supplement its existing supplies.

In Classical Greece running water, whether from a local spring or conveyed through an aqueduct from a distant source, was usually regarded as communal property. True the 10-mile (16-km.) long conduit built in the fifth century B.C. to serve the city of Olynthus did give an individual supply to a few privileged houses lying along the route to the public fountains, but this was very much an exception to the rule. Generally the only private sources of water were wells and rainwater cisterns, and most families relied on fountains erected by their town authorities. Great care was lavished on such fountains, which were often protected by a colonnaded building and provided with several decorative spouts constantly gushing water. Women

A vase-painting showing Greek women visiting a public fountain.

who came to fill their jugs stayed to gossip, making the fountain house one
of the great social centres of the ancient Greek city.

Once the water was carried home, usually in a vessel poised gracefully
on the head, it was used not only for drinking and cooking but also for
personal hygiene. The Greeks were a cleanly people who washed and bathed
regularly. Usually they scrubbed themselves down while standing before a
shallow bowl mounted on a pedestal; more occasionally they knelt or
squatted in a round bath resembling a gigantic pudding basin.

Of all ancient civilizations Rome paid the greatest attention to water
supply. The parent city itself was eventually provided with thirteen aqueducts while even a minor provincial town like Lincoln in Britain had a
distribution system linked by pipe-line to a spring over a mile outside the
walls. In all Roman cities, however, most of the water went either to public
baths or the municipal fountains, and little to private consumers, since only
the rich could afford the sizable fee charged for the privilege of a direct
connection to the mains. The numerous flat-dwelling inhabitants of Rome
itself were particularly unfortunate in the matter of water. If poverty did
not deny them access to a piped supply, then the height of their tenement
home probably did. Great plumbers though the Romans were, they seldom 105

A Greek youth bathing.

ran water pipes into the upper storeys of even the grandest buildings, let alone those of slumland flats. When the flat-dweller wanted water he had either to fetch it from the street fountain himself or employ a water-carrier to do the job for him. In fact the water-carriers who served a block of flats loomed so large in its corporate life that Roman lawyers were of the opinion that they should be transferred automatically to the new owner when the building changed hands. Water carried so painstakingly to upstairs flats was naturally used very sparingly. Fortunately, however, there was no need for anyone to go dirty, for Rome and its more important colonial towns were well endowed with public baths.

Though only the wealthy had water piped into their houses, the Roman authorities had ensured that there was more than enough for all at the public fountains and baths. This era of copious organized supply came to an end over most of Europe with the fall of the Roman Empire in the West. Rome's own conduits were severed by the besieging Goths in A.D. 537; in many of her former provinces the aqueducts and pipe-lines were either smashed by barbarian invaders or allowed to fall into disrepair. People turned once more to the age-old sources of spring and river.

In the East, however, Roman power survived and efficient water distribution continued. The imperial capital had been transferred to Constantinople (formerly Byzantium) in A.D. 330, so that Rome had lost much of its central importance long before it fell into barbarian hands. Various emperors took a part in the provision of water for the new capital. Constantine, its founder, dammed up several springs to make reservoirs from which the public fountains could be supplied. When these original sources had been outgrown Valens (A.D. 364–378) constructed the aqueduct that can still be seen in modern Istanbul. A second aqueduct was provided by Theodosius I towards the end of the fourth century. Water collected from the various sources was fed into four large open tanks partly to allow suspended matter to settle but also, no doubt, to furnish an adequate reserve in case the city were attacked and its conduits cut. The open reservoirs fed a number of remarkable underground tanks, which with their many columns and vaulted roofs resemble submerged cathedrals. Antioch, the second city of the Eastern Empire, was also provided with an abundant supply of water. Its principal aqueduct was particularly impressive, marching across valleys on the usual bridge-like structures which at one point rose to the height of 200 feet (61 m.).

After the worst of the chaos that followed the fall of Rome had subsided a new Europe of petty kingdoms began to emerge. The old political unity had gone and only the Church retained its international outlook. Significantly it was the men of religion, with their roots still in the Roman past, who hesitatingly began to re-establish artificial supplies.

One of the first signs of slowly improving standards was the partial

Reconstruction of the aqueducts supplying ancient Rome.

restoration of Rome's supply by Pope Adrian I, who in 776 ordered that underground conduits be substituted for some broken sections of the old overhead aqueducts. But naturally enough most of these early church enterprises were designed primarily to bring water into religious houses. This was certainly the case with the works undertaken in the ninth century by the priories of St. Laurent and St. Lazare near Paris, though when the monks had succeeded in tapping several nearby springs they did have the generosity to supply two public fountains with the water surplus to their own needs. In Britain the channels dug by St. Aethelwald in the tenth century to bring water to the religious establishments of Winchester were incidentally of benefit to the townspeople.

But such additions to existing supplies were rare indeed until considerably later times. William Fitzstephen, for instance, writing of the London he knew in the twelfth century, makes it clear that the city relied on the 'sweet, clear, and salubrious' waters of its natural springs. It was not until 1237 that, in the words of John Stow the sixteenth-century antiquarian,

> '. . . the fresh waters that were in and about the city, being in process of time, by incroachment for buildings and heightenings of grounds, utterly decayed, and the number of citizens mightily increased, they were forced to seek sweet waters abroad. . . .'

Fortunately the king, Henry III, came to the help of the Londoners at their moment of need, and persuaded Gilbert Sanforde, Lord of the Manor of Tyburn, to allow the construction of a six-inch (15-cm.) lead pipe or conduit to carry water from the springs on his property into the city at Cheapside.

Gradually the demand for fresh water was felt in other towns. Some people helped themselves. Before the thirteenth century was out the citizens of Dublin had constructed a conduit to supply their street fountains, while the inhabitants of Hull had increased their supply by diverting a spring into the bed of an existing stream. Others looked to the Church for help and were often fortunate. During the fourteenth century such English cities as Southampton, Chester, Grantham, and Lincoln all gained a share in the water piped to local monasteries.

Medieval conduits did not, of course, carry water into the individual houses of ordinary people. Instead the pipes led directly to communal conduit heads or fountains from which the water had to be fetched. As in ancient Rome, many citizens seem to have found this such a hardship that they were prepared to employ professional carriers to do the job for them. The trade grew as burghers became more prosperous, and as early as 1292

Paris supported fifty-eight water-sellers. To avoid either the expense of buying or the labour of fetching, the unscrupulous were sometimes tempted to tap into the public conduits with branch pipes of their own, but this practice was frowned upon as highly anti-social. A record of 1478 describes the apt punishment meted out to William Campion, a Londoner caught out in the offence. Mounted on horseback he was paraded ignominiously through the streets while water cascaded all over him from the holes in a constantly replenished vessel perched on his head. The only legitimate private supplies within a city were likely to be those to a monastery or a royal palace.

Out in the country the great houses and castles of the nobility were invariably sited near a good source of water. The minimum requirement was a reliable well, but a natural spring was better still. Sometimes a stream was diverted into a channel leading to the kitchen. In early castles like the Tower of London and Colchester the well-head was frequently in the basement, but this inconvenient arrangement was avoided in some later buildings by carrying the shaft up in the thickness of the wall so that water could be delivered to each floor through openings at the appropriate levels. The twelfth-century castle at Newcastle-upon-Tyne went one better, and, by

Medieval wall-basin in Battle Hall, Leeds, Kent.

means of a system of gulleys running from basins on either side of the second-floor well-head, distributed water to various parts of the keep. Caernarvon Castle, built between 1283 and 1323, had a somewhat similar set up. Water drawn from the well was emptied into a lead-lined cistern from which stone channels ran off to the kitchen and other strategic points.

A good deal of the water used in the Middle Ages was required for straightforward consumption or, as John Stow put it, 'for the poor to drink, and the rich to dress their meat'. But this was far from the whole story. Great quantities were employed in the production of a weak ale, which was so cheap that few but the very poor drank plain water. Surprising amounts were also devoted, at least by the upper classes, to personal hygiene. The medieval baron was by no means the unscrubbed ruffian of popular imagination. Etiquette demanded that at very least he wash his hands and face and rinse his teeth on rising in the morning—a custom which explains the existence of the stone wall-basins found in many medieval houses. Probably a water container of some sort originally hung over most such sinks. A very developed form, complete with tap, is shown in a woodcut made by Albrecht Dürer in 1509.

Besides the morning ablutions people of quality were expected to wash

A wash-stand shown in a medieval miniature.

Early sixteenth-century washing arrangements from a print by Albrecht Dürer.

before and during meals, for in those days, prior to the adoption of forks, fingers were used to pick up the food. Between courses a server attended table with a bowl and ewer, pouring a little water over each diner's outstretched hands. Another server followed behind bearing a towel. This genteel picture is, however, somewhat marred by the warnings in the *Book of Curtasye* against cleaning one's teeth on the table cloth and spitting 'over the borde or elles opone'.

Water was also used for bathing. King John is said to have taken a bath every three weeks and, judging by the trouble his successors took to equip bathrooms, they must have indulged even more frequently. John's grandson, Edward I, impressed no doubt by what he had seen in the East, ordered a modernization of the bathing arrangements at the Palace of Westminster within a year of his return from the last Crusade in 1274. The 'laver' (washbasin) in the bathroom was to be supplied with running water controlled by a tap, while the 'baynes' (baths) themselves were to be fitted with four taps of gilt bronze. Probably the piped supply was originally unheated, 111

This fifteenth-century painting, **One of Three Legends of St Nicholas,** *shows the type of wooden bath which had been typical since medieval times.*

but Edward III's accounts reveal that in 1351 two new taps were bought, one for hot water and one for cold. This was most unusual. Baths were commonly filled by hand with water heated in a cauldron.

Medieval bath-tubs seem almost invariably to have been made from wooden staves after the manner of barrels. Sometimes the tubs were circular but often they were elongated to make room for several bathers at once. People in those days were not embarrassed by nudity, and heated water was not to be wasted. The fashion for bathing spread downwards through most of society. The king had his fitted bathroom; the noble his tub before the bedroom fire; even the poor townsman with no means of heating large quantities of water at home could visit one of the many public stews which had sprung up in the wake of the crusades. Only the agricultural worker seems to have been left out in the cold.

By the end of the Middle Ages baths had grown less popular. Henry VIII attempted to close down the public stews on the grounds that they were notorious haunts of immorality, while his daughter Elizabeth I was considered eccentric for the monthly bath which she took 'whether she need it or no'. But despite this decline in cleanliness, the overall demand for water rose as the cities grew ever more populous. By the end of the sixteenth century London had at least sixteen conduits and this was still not enough. Fortunately, however, technology came to the rescue. Waterwheels could be set in the arches of a bridge so using a river's own power to pump its waters into the city fountains. The loss in quality was serious because rivers were already heavily polluted, but the increase in quantity was so great that for the first time water could be piped into the houses of quite ordinary people. Breslau erected a waterwheel in 1479; Toledo in 1526; Augsburg followed in 1548. John Stow records that Thames water was conveyed 'into men's houses by pipes of lead from a most artificial forcier standing near unto London bridge, and made by Peter Moris, Dutchman, in the year 1582, for service of the city, on the east part thereof'. During the seventeenth century waterworks of this kind were established in many other European towns.

The Thames at London Bridge was obviously contaminated even in the early seventeenth century, and in 1606 the corporation obtained parliamentary permission for the construction of a canal to bring Hertfordshire spring waters into the city. Fearful of the difficulties, however, the Common Council hesitated to start on the project, which would have been abandoned altogether but for the faith of goldsmith Hugh Myddelton, who undertook the work at his own risk. Expenses did indeed prove very high, and at one point Myddelton faced financial ruin, only to be rescued by a timely offer of partnership from James I. The 38-mile (61-km.) long New River, starting from Chadwell and terminating in a reservoir at Clerkenwell, was completed in 1613, and by November 1614 water was being delivered to some of the City streets. Water distribution was entering its modern phase. The editors of the posthumous version of Stow's *Survey of London*, published in 1633, were ecstatic about the improvements:

> 'What with the spring-water coming from several springheads through the streets of the city to these cisterns, the New River water from Chadwell and Anwell, and the Thames water raised by several engines or water-houses, there is not a street in London but one or other of these waters runs through it in pipes conveyed underground; and from these pipes there is scarce a house whose rent is £15 or £20 a year, but hath the convenience of water brought into it by small leaden pipes laid into the great ones. And for the smaller tenements, such as are in courts and alleys, there is generally a cock or pump common to the inhabitants; so that I may boldly say, there is never a city in the world so well served with water.'

But the supply picture was not so rosy as this account would have us believe. The annual rate charged by the various water companies was very high in terms of the money values of the day and the service offered decidedly restricted. The New River Company, for instance, charged a householder the yearly sum of 26s. 8d. to supply one tap in the kitchen and another in the yard through a half-inch pipe. To make matters worse, running water was only available for a few hours every day, during which time storage cisterns had to be recharged to last through the dry period. It is also certain that at first only the wealthier Londoners enjoyed even this limited service, for water-carriers remained active in the capital until the eighteenth century.

Although piped water gradually became available to a wider public, washing habits showed little change. The genteel toilette centred round basin and water jug, and although the face and hands were rinsed with reasonable regularity the rest of the body received little attention. Ordinary people often simply washed at the pump. Bathing was a rare luxury in which few indulged at home. There were, however, public 'hot houses' where the accumulated layers of filth could be sweated away. Samuel Pepys recorded that his wife visited such an establishment 'after her long being within doors in the dirt', but doubted her resolution 'of being hereafter very clean'. As late as 1801 a doctor complained that although most Londoners washed daily they went for years without a bath.

Several technological advances helped to increase the domestic supply of water still further during the eighteenth century. In 1712 one of Savery's newly invented engines for 'raising water by fire' was installed at London's York Buildings waterworks. The experiment was quickly abandoned because of exorbitant fuel bills, but it pointed the way to the future. Undeterred by this initial failure the same company tried out a Newcomen steam engine in 1726, persevering for five years until costs again forced them to return to horse-driven pumps. In 1742 another London company, the Chelsea Water Works, achieved success with an improved Newcomen and other water

A seventeenth-century lady washing her hands using basin and jug.

This Rowlandson cartoon shows the type of water supply provided for the kitchens of wealthy households in the eighteenth century. Note the large storage tank dated 1730.

concerns in London, the provinces, and abroad were gradually won over by the reliability and power of steam. The London Bridge Water Works supplemented its river-driven wheels with a steam engine in about 1762, so that output could be maintained during slack water periods. York acquired a steam engine in 1784, and Hull in 1795. Paris dramatically increased its supply by bringing two steam-pumps into action in 1781. Figures issued eleven years later show that these two pumps alone were responsible for nearly three-quarters of the French capital's supply. The first steam-driven machinery to be installed in an American waterworks was commissioned by the Watering Committee of Philadelphia in 1797.

But more powerful and reliable pumps were not the only requirement for improved services. The hollowed-out tree trunks used as street mains by the early water companies had proved notoriously leaky and quick to rot. Vast quantities of valuable water were lost before ever reaching the consumers. High pressures were also impossible so that storage cisterns had usually to be situated on the ground floor or in the basement, and water pumped or carried to higher levels. Better mains were clearly essential. Earthenware was tried and found wanting; then attention focused on cast iron. Small-scale experiments with cast-iron pipes were undertaken in several towns both in France and Britain from the mid-eighteenth century onwards, but the breakthrough came in about 1785 with Thomas Simpson's invention of the spigot and socket joint. It now became possible to cast comparatively short lengths of pipe and join them successfully together. In 1811 the New River Company, London's largest undertaking at that time, decided to change from wood to cast iron. The Metropolis Paving Act of 1817 further stimulated the spread of cast-iron mains by its insistence that all new pipes laid in the capital should be made from that metal. Philadelphia began to import British cast-iron mains in the same year but other American towns were slower to respond. Boston did not replace its pine-log pipes until 1846, while Chicago kept its for five years longer. It was only when water companies learnt to combine stronger mains with more powerful pumps that it became possible to provide piped supplies to upper storeys and loft cisterns.

Innovation was not entirely limited to the supply side. The ball valve, first mentioned in print in 1748, freed the householder from a minor but irksome chore. Previous to its invention the flow of water into the storage cistern had to be controlled by tap and someone had to remember to turn off before the tank overflowed. Many a home must have run dry or been flooded because a careless servant forgot to turn the tap. Early ball valves might have been rather leaky and prone to go wrong, but they were less fallible than human memory.

Technology had provided the key to a copious supply of water for everyone but society was not yet ready to make use of it to the full. The report issued in 1844 by the Health of Towns Commission, set up by the British Government, revealed that out of the fifty towns investigated only six had good water supplies while thirty-one had distinctly bad. There was an almost universal lack of piped water in the homes of the poorer sections of the community, and in London alone 300,000 out of the 900,000 people in the New River Company's area were 'unsupplied'. Some large manufacturing

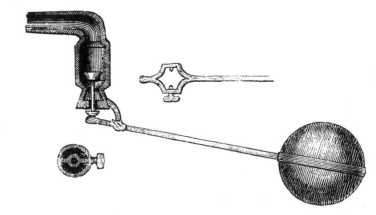

The type of ball valve used in the mid-nineteenth century.

towns were even worse off, with whole districts reliant on water sold from water-carts at $\frac{1}{2}$d. or 1d. per bucket. Of those fortunate enough to receive a piped supply many enjoyed only an intermittent service. At York, for instance, half the houses supplied received water for two hours on Mondays, Wednesdays, and Fridays; the remainder got theirs on Tuesdays, Thursdays, and Saturdays. On Sundays the whole town went dry. Conditions were no better abroad. Water-sellers were still active in Paris, while the growing city of New York had been completely dependent on well- and river-water until the completion of the Croton aqueduct in 1842.

In many towns the quality of the water also gave serious grounds for concern. As early as 1827 a pamphlet entitled *The Dolphin* had attacked the water supplied by the Grand Junction Water Works Company to 7,000 houses in Westminster as 'Offensive to the sight, Disgusting to the imagination and Destructive to the Health'. These allegations were well founded for the company's intake was within a few yards of the Ranelagh sewer. Following a public outcry this situation was partially remedied by a transfer of the intake up-river, but less obvious abuses continued unchecked. Many homes were being supplied with what was virtually sewage.

Such a state of affairs could not long continue without a dreadful retribution. In the 1830s Europe and America were visited by the scourge of Asiatic cholera. Thousands died before the epidemic receded. The 1840s experienced another outbreak and during the summer months of 1849 between 200 and 400 Londoners died from the disease every day. It was not lost on careful observers that the worst affected areas were those which drew their water from the heavily polluted lower reaches of the Thames. Districts served by purer sources or with water filtered through sand-beds in the way pioneered by the Chelsea company twenty years previously suffered far less heavily. For years reformers had been preaching the need for better water supplies; now they received general support. Parliament responded with the Metropolis Water Act of 1852, forbidding companies to draw water from the Thames below Teddington Lock and ordering them to filter all river-derived water, whatever the source. These laws, though not fully implemented as far as filtration was concerned until the 1870s, marked the beginning of modern hygienic water practice.

Progress was also being made in extending the availability of supply. Intermittent services were giving way to continuous, and piped water was beginning to flow into even the poorest homes. Joseph Parry, writing in his *Practical Handbook on Water* in 1881, could claim that 'there is no town (in Britain) of importance without public works from which water is distributed through pipes to every dwelling'. The age of Aquarius had arrived.

The water was there, but for long the best use was not made of it. Many landlords were too mean to install more than the bare minimum of fittings and many tenants were woefully ignorant of the benefits of hygiene. When Parry praised the provision of a 'separate tap in each house', it is significant that he used the singular. The solitary tap over the kitchen sink had to suffice for all the household needs of many a working-class family well into the twentieth century. Back in the 1880s some people were even unfamiliar with the use of ordinary screw-down stopcocks. Parry tells the story of a water-board engineer who called at a house and was asked to look at a defective tap. 'It has been here about a year,' complained the housewife, 'and scarcely any water will come out of it, and it's always leaking.' The engineer could discover nothing wrong with the tap, but his puzzlement turned to amusement when he realized that the woman had thought it one of the old-fashioned plug variety, and so had never turned it properly on or off.

The portable bath, hand filled and hand emptied, survived well into the era of high pressure mains when piped water could easily have been delivered to any room in the house. Cost was partly responsible for this state of affairs, but a reluctance to accept new standards and ideas was also an important factor. Many quite wealthy people, who could well have afforded the necessary plumbing, hesitated to install a fixed bath. S. S. Hellyer, the

Selection of wash-basins from the 1899 Twyfords catalogue.

famous sanitarian, wrote in his *The Plumber and Sanitary Houses* published in 1877 that 'one may as well look for a fountain in a desert as for a bath in any of our old English houses'. But attitudes were changing, for in a footnote to the 1884 edition Hellyer could add that 'no new house now in London and the suburbs is considered complete without this modern "luxury"'. He was, of course referring to middle-class housing only.

Hand-in-hand with the slow adoption of the bathroom came the gradual abandonment of the old-fashioned wash-stand, jug, and bowl in favour of the upstairs wash-basin served by running hot and cold water. Wash-basins fitted with taps had appeared in the trade catalogues of the 1850s, but, since at that time a hand pump was nearly always required to raise the water needed for their supply, they had gained little popularity. It was not until the 1870s that the wash-basin really caught on, and then only with the moneyed classes. Early wash-basins were more like elaborate pieces of furniture than plumbing fittings. Their slab marble tops and pipe-hiding mahogany enclosures made them prohibitively expensive for all but the very rich. After about 1880 a much cheaper variety, using a cast-iron framework to support an earthenware bowl, came on to the market. One-piece whiteware basins very similar to those in use today appeared at the beginning of the present century.

The bathrooms of the 1870s and 1880s, being made for the extremely wealthy, established a pattern of unnecessarily ostentatious splendour. Stained-glass windows, a profusion of carved woodwork, and a tiled floor all combined to give an almost church-like atmosphere. This style was at

A bathroom of 1853 from an advertisement in The Builder.

A bathroom of 1904.

first imitated by the middle class, but inevitably designs tended to become more functional as purse strings grew tighter. For a start, the rich wooden panelling surrounding the tub was gradually made redundant by new manufacturing techniques. After about 1880 cast iron began to replace sheet metal in bath construction, and by the late 1890s the free-standing model, often with a decorative finish applied to the outside, had become acceptable. Stripped of superfluous detail the bathroom shrank to something like its present cell-like proportions. Just prior to the 1914–18 war the perfection of the porcelain-enamelling process enabled a much longer-lasting surface to be applied to metal. Good quality baths, porcelain-enamelled within and painted without, now became available at prices which ordinary people could afford. After the war there was a great and continuing boom in sales and between 1930 and 1937 the number of British houses possessing bathrooms doubled. Even today, however, in the affluent Britain of the early seventies one and a half million households lack a bath of their own. The provision of such essentials has yet to match the excellence of the water service, so long perfected and so reliable that it is almost taken for granted.

6

A Place Without

Domestic sanitation is both a product and a requirement of advanced civilization. Life in the closely packed houses and flats of a great modern city would be unbearable without an effective means of sewage disposal. In primitive times the need for elaborate sanitary arrangements was far less pressing. While man was nomadic or lived only in very small communities, common sense was all that was required to keep the environment healthy. Space was wide, people were few, and bushes were plenty. The practice recommended to the ancient Hebrews in the twenty-third chapter of Deuteronomy must have been followed unknowingly by many less literate peoples all over the world.

> 'Thou shalt have a place also without the camp, whither thou shalt go forth abroad:
> And thou shalt have a paddle upon thy weapon; and it shall be when thou wilt ease thyself abroad, thou shalt dig therewith, and shalt turn back and cover that which cometh from thee.'

Permanent villages were more difficult to keep clean than nomadic camps. After a few years' continuous occupation, the land close around became excessively fouled. Houses, however, were flimsy affairs, and were due for rebuilding by the time the surroundings had become unpleasant. What more sensible, then, than to move the whole village? In England there are many known cases of early Saxon settlements being abandoned after a short occupation only to be re-established within a few hundred yards of their original sites. The Saxon found it easier to move himself than his sewage. In modern Africa a similar expedient is still sometimes followed, and after four or five years in one spot the village is dismantled and rebuilt on fresh ground nearby.

With the advent of cities about 5,500 years ago, time-honoured sanitary methods became outdated. It was too far to walk to the bushes and an entire city could hardly be shifted every time it got a trifle smelly. New techniques were required if the urban house was to be kept sweet and whole-some. The different civilizations have met with varying success in their endeavours to find a solution to this sanitary problem. Some let dungheaps accumulate and put up with the consequences; others carted their wastes out of town for use as manure on the fields; a few developed sewers.

Amongst the carters, perhaps the most ingenious were the Aztecs of the Mexico City area who used what could be called 'mobile sewers'. Before they were demoralized by the Spanish Conquest of the early sixteenth century these people moored special 'lavatory boats' along the banks of the many waterways which intersected their island city. When full, the boats were simply towed away and handed over to the farmers. Across the world in Japan human wastes were an important item of trade for hundreds of years after the fall of the Aztec empire. Each house collected the valuable commodity in a cesspit built directly under the plain hole in the floor which acted as the privy. In the country the contents were simply bucketed out and carried straight to the fields, but in town the ordure was taken to waiting barges for shipment to the farms.

Carting even survived in some English provincial towns until the early years of the present century. Every week the slop cart, a great open tank on wheels, lurched its way through the back streets. Each privy was invaded, its wooden tub seized in metal tongs, emptied with a splash, and pushed back into position. Often the contents spilt out on to the road and even the passage of a cart spraying carbolic disinfectant could not quite wipe out either the smell or the traces. Affairs had been much better contrived in a number of ancient cities.

As long as four thousand years ago a high proportion of the houses in the great Indus Valley towns of Mohenjo-daro and Harappā were equipped with water-flushed latrines discharging into the street drains. Although these channels were open, they were well constructed and easily scoured out by a flow of water. As a means of city cleansing they were certainly superior to the slop cart.

Closed sewers are just as old and seem to have been invented in Mesopo-tamia. The sewers of several Mesopotamian palaces of the latter part of the third millennium B.C. have been unearthed. Excavators at Eshnunna have even found the remains of the large jars which once stood beside each royal privy to provide flushing-water. Gradually the sanitary idea caught on and by about 1800 B.C., when the houses investigated by Sir Leonard Woolley at Ur were being built, most wealthy merchants had come to consider a latrine connected to a terracotta sewer as a domestic necessity. Drainage, however, never penetrated into the poorer quarters of the 123

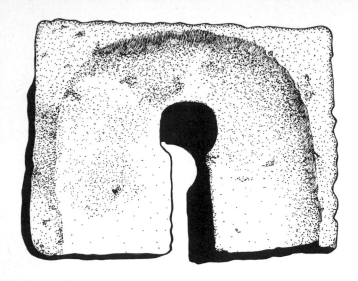

A limestone lavatory seat from ancient Egypt.

Mesopotamian city.

In the matter of drains the richest of ancient Egyptians was no better off than the humblest of his Mesopotamian contemporaries. For all its other accomplishments the mighty civilization of Egypt never developed sewers, and even the divine Pharaoh had to make do with an earth closet. Several privies have been discovered at Tell-el-Amarna, the site of the briefly occupied capital established by the heretic Pharaoh Akhenaten during the fourteenth century B.C. Akhenaten conceived the novel idea of replacing the multitude of Egyptian gods with one all-embracing divinity, but his new city contained no corresponding innovations in sanitation. The latrines were strictly traditional with a removable container placed beneath the seat. No water was used for cleansing, though it seems probable that the box-like depressions on either side of one privy were stores from which dried earth could be taken and sprinkled in after each use. Limestone seats seem to have been a popular status symbol. One pierced by a curious keyhole-shaped opening has been recovered intact. Lesser mortals made do with a wooden plank supported between two bricks.

Egyptian backwardness in sanitary matters is all the more surprising when contrasted with the skill of the Minoans of island Crete—the acknowledged master plumbers of the ancient world. Minoan trading vessels thronged the ports of the Nile, but although tales about the marvels of the Palace of Minos must have reached the Egyptians, they chose to pay no heed. Perhaps, as the inhabitants of a land where the rainfall was so scanty that not even the simplest run-off channel was required, they found the notion of underground drains too far outside their experience to seem credible and dismissed the self-cleansing lavatory as just another sailor's yarn.

But the accomplishments of the Minoans were real enough. Their engineers seemed to revel in constructing pipes, building water channels, and digging drains. From about 1700 B.C. the palace at Knossos was provided with an outstanding drainage system—small drains emptying into huge, stone-lined sewers big enough for a workman to pass through with ease. One of the lavatories connected to this elaborate system has been identified as belonging to the queen herself. Traces of a wooden seat and arrangements for flushing with water show the whole set-up to have been surprisingly modernistic in both concept and appearance.

Knossos was destroyed by invaders from the Greek mainland, probably in the aftermath of an earthquake which took place in about 1400 B.C., and the secrets of its plumbing were forgotten. The Greeks never recovered the lost art, and although their civilization waxed great during the sixth and fifth centuries B.C. their sanitation remained primitive. Rome, whose power engulfed the Mediterranean world during the second century B.C., was a much worthier heir to Minos than Athens had ever been.

As with other peoples, the Romans seem to have been helped in their development of sewers by their earlier experience with rain-water channels. The principal sewer of their city, the Cloaca Maxima, began as an open ditch dug during the sixth century B.C. to drain the marshy area which eventually became the Forum. Gradually the function of the cloaca was extended. Household drains were led into it, and by the time it was vaulted over, about two hundred years after its inception, it had become a true sewer. During the second century B.C. it was paved with blocks of lava and reconstructed so thoroughly that much of it has survived to the present day.

In size and cleanliness the cloaca was truly impressive. It was large enough to allow the passage of a small boat, and was constantly dredged by slaves and scoured by the outflow of water from the numerous public baths and fountains. There was only one major deficiency. Few, if any, of the flats in which the ordinary Romans lived were connected to this fine system of sewers. During the day lack of private sanitation was no great inconvenience. Rome possessed many spacious public latrines with rows of stone seats built over channels of swiftly flowing water. The décor was usually attractive, some establishments boasting statues and fountains, and few people seem to have begrudged the small entrance fee. Public lavatories became favourite social gathering places where friends met and chatted without embarrassment. A completely free sanitary service was provided by the fullers. They required urine for their trade, and to collect it placed outside their shops special pots which, in those uninhibited times, were readily filled by passers-by. But at night, when the flat-dweller had retired, his only recourse was 125

A fifteenth-century latrine built between houses.

to the chamber pot. Home-going revellers had to beware a deluge from above, for many householders emptied such vessels out of the window rather than face the morning trudge down to the cess-tank at the foot of the stairs, or the dungheap in the neighbouring alley.

Wealthy Romans were much better off. Their city mansions enjoyed the full benefits of main drainage, and some of their privies were even flushed from above in a very modern manner. The ornate, marble-clad latrine in the Palace of the Caesars contained a cistern from which water was distributed by cocks to the various seats. There were, however, limitations to Roman sanitary skill. Little if any attempt was made to prevent sewer gases escaping into the house, while the health-giving properties of air and light seem often to have been ignored. It was a common practice in more modest establishments to situate the privy in an unventilated alcove just off the kitchen—presumably so that the expense of separate kitchen and lavatory drains could be avoided.

Sewers and drains were not confined to the imperial capital alone. They were introduced widely throughout the empire and have been traced beneath the towns of even such an outlying province as Britain. Lincoln, where each of the principal streets had a stone-built sewer big enough for a man to crawl through, had a particularly elaborate system. Other centres, like Verulamium (St. Albans), possessed at least some sewers of comparable size. The Roman world achieved sanitary standards unrivalled until the nineteenth century, but after its collapse farm-yard practices quickly re-established themselves. Conditions were far too unsettled in the western Europe of the fifth and sixth centuries for any of the niceties of urban life to survive.

Only very gradually did Europe return to some sort of political stability as the invading barbarians carved out new kingdoms from the old Roman provinces. It was not until the eleventh century that towns began to blossom once more, and by then the arts of sanitation had virtually been forgotten. Most medieval townsmen kept cattle or pigs and thought it natural to add human wastes to the pile of manure ripening beside cow-shed or sty. City dungheaps were for long tolerated as inevitable, though citizens were expected to have the muck carted out of town before too much accumulated. William Wigger of St. Ives was actually hauled before the courts in 1302 and fined sixpence for obstructing the street with an outsized pile of garbage and manure. An illustration from a fifteenth-century copy of the *Decameron* shows that it was sometimes the custom for a latrine to be built out from the upper storey of a house so as to project over a dungheap below.

Practices like this represent medieval sanitation at its worst. Andrew Boorde, who died in 1549, was drawing on much sounder traditions when he advised that 'the common house of easement be over some water or else elongated from the house'. 'Elongated', in this instance, usually meant a privy built above a cesspit in the yard or garden. Cesspools seem to have been used from quite early in the Middle Ages, and were perhaps the best method of sewage disposal that could be achieved with the limited technical resources of the times. They were specifically mentioned in the building regulations issued to Londoners in 1189 which forbad the digging of cess-pits within $5\frac{1}{2}$ feet (1·7 m.) of a neighbour's property, if they were to be unwalled, or $2\frac{1}{2}$ feet (76 cm.), if they were to be lined with stone.

Boorde's alternative piece of advice was of more dubious value. For centuries before his time it had been the habit of those living beside streams and rivers to build privies out over the water. In this way such people were certainly spared the trouble of dealing with their wastes, but only at the expense of polluting the waters which they and others had to drink. London's lesser rivers, like the Fleet, had long been converted into open sewers when the city authorities belatedly and probably ineffectually banned latrines over the minor waterways in 1477. Other cities allowed their streams to become tainted in exactly the same way. Artificial closed sewers were a great rarity during the medieval era, though short lengths were occasionally constructed to drain houses belonging to wealthy noblemen.

Great houses and castles often had an entire block or even a tower devoted to sanitary purposes. Latrines were constructed on each of the upper floors, and shafts led down to ground level. Here, however, there was a return to the primitive. In the absence of a conveniently sited stream, the shafts usually discharged either directly into the stagnant waters of the moat or into a cesspit which was probably not cleaned out more than once a year. Sanitary towers were sometimes large enough to serve a dual purpose. The latrines were partitioned off and the remaining space was used as a wardrobe for hanging clothes—hence the euphemism 'garderobe' for the medieval privy.

The best sanitary arrangements of the Middle Ages were to be found in the houses of the monastic orders. Sites were chosen and buildings laid out so as to ensure that a stream passed beneath the monk's latrine to carry away the sewage. The sanitary block with its long row of cubicles customarily formed a wing of the dormitory or 'dorter' and was consequently known as the 'reredorter'. One abbot at St. Albans actually carried cleanliness to what was probably regarded as an eccentric level. Not content to have the odour of sanctity carried off downstream he erected a stone rainwater cistern

Medieval garderobes in a tower of the bishop's palace at Southwell, Nottinghamshire.

to enable his own private latrine to be flushed from above.

The worst features of medieval sanitation persisted even when new ideas began to permeate through western Europe awakening a fresh interest in learning. The upsurge of the Renaissance during the fifteenth century transformed men's minds but did little for their privies. Cesspits and dungheaps remained for most people an inevitable if unwelcome adjunct to life. For some they also spelled death, usually through the insidious spread of disease, but occasionally in a spectacular manner as when in 1498 no less a person than George Pfeffer von Hell, Chancellor of the Electorate at Mentz, fell into a cesspool and was drowned. It took a genius of the stature of Leonardo da Vinci (1452–1519) to transcend the contemporary acceptance of filth and make the radical suggestion that all urban privies should drain into underground sewers discharging into the local river. Like so many of Leonardo's ideas, however, this one was recorded in his notebooks but, if revealed in his lifetime, ignored.

A less exalted but nevertheless talented son of the Renaissance was slightly more successful in his attempts at sanitary reform. This was Sir John Harington, a godson of Queen Elizabeth I, who in 1596 wrote a book playfully entitled *The Metamorphosis of Ajax* (a pun on the vulgar work 'jakes'), extolling in ribald terms the virtues of his newly invented water closet. In his enthusiasm he dared to go so far as to suggest that it 'may be beneficiall not only to my private friends, but to townes and cities, yea even to her Majesties service for some of her houses'. The Queen was furious at this impudence and banished Sir John from court. Nothing dismayed, the incautious knight, whose wit had landed him in trouble before, set himself to win back his sovereign's favour and met with such success that eventually the Queen allowed him to install a water closet at her palace of Richmond in Surrey. It may be that a previous first-hand experience had something to do with Elizabeth's change of heart for she had visited Sir John's home at Kelston near Bath in 1592 and if the famous privy had already been installed would certainly have used it.

What was remarkable about Harington's invention was the complete way in which it anticipated the essential features of a modern hygienic toilet. It had flushing from above, but that cleansing technique had occasionally been used since the times of Minoan Crete. Much more important was the use of a valve and a water-seal to prevent foul sewer gases escaping through the privy into the house. An extract from *The Metamorphosis of Ajax* shows that Sir John had a clear understanding of the problem his closet was intended to solve. 'For there be,' he wrote, 'few great & well contrived houses, but have vaults and secret passages made under ground, to convey away

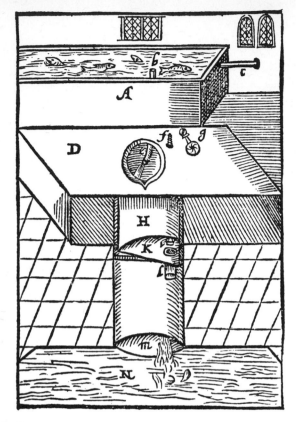

A. the Cesterne.
B. the little washer.
C. the wast pipe.
D. the seate boord.
E. the pipe that comes from the Cesterne.
F. the Screw.
G. the Scallop shell to cover it when it is shut downe.[53]
H. the stoole pot.
I. the stopple.
K. the current.
L. the sluce.[54]
M. N. the vault into which it falles: always remember that at noone
and at night, emptie it and leave it halfe a foote deepe in fayre water.
And this being well done, and orderly kept, your worst privie may
be as sweet as your best chamber.

both the ordure & other noisome things, as also the raine water that falles
into the courts, which being cleanly in respect of the eye, yet because they
must of force have many vents, they are oft noisome in regard of the smell.
Specially in houses of office, that stand high from the ground, the tuns of
them drawing up the aire as a chimney doth smoke.'

Harington's solution was to seal the privy except when it was being voided
into the vault or sewer below. The seat was arranged above a vertical, oval-
sectioned pipe some 2 feet (61 cm.) long which was closed off about half-way

down by a partition sloping towards the right. A brass outlet pipe, $2\frac{1}{2}$ inches (6·35 cm.) in diameter, passed through the partition at its lowest point to allow the contents of the privy to empty. Normally this pipe was kept stoppered by a valve on the end of a rod which extended up through a small hole in the seat. The end of the rod was threaded so that with a few turns of a special key the valve could be raised or securely tightened into position. As an added precaution to ensure 'no ayre come up from the vault', the user of the closet was instructed that 'ever it must be left, after it is voyded, halfe a foote deepe in cleane water'. The privy was completed by the provision of a cistern 'containing a barrell or upward, to be placed either behind the seat, or in any place, either in the room, or above it, from whence the water may by a small pype of leade of an inch be convayed under the seate in the hinder part therof (but not quite out of sight) to which pype you must have a Cocke or a washer to yeeld water with some pretie strength, when you would let it in.'

Perhaps if sewers had been more freely available Harington's invention would have enjoyed some lasting success. As it was it left the problem of the final disposal of sewage quite untouched. Water for flushing would also have been a difficulty since in those days few houses enjoyed the luxury of a piped supply. Whatever the reasons the water closet did not take on and the whole idea seems to have been completely forgotten within a few years. Samuel Pepys writing around the middle of the next century seemed quite content with 'a very fine close stool' and a cesspit in the cellar.

Water closets were not heard of again until John Aubrey described one at Sir Francis Carew's house at Beddington in Surrey. The account first appeared in Aubrey's discourse on that county, published posthumously in 1719, but must actually have been written at some time before 1697, when the author died. What he saw was 'a pretty machine to cleanse an "House of Office", viz., by a small stream of water no bigger than one's finger, which ran into an engine made like a bit of fire-shovel, which hung upon its centre of gravity, so that when it was full a considerable quantity of water fell down with some force and washed away the filth'. It is clear from this description that the 'engine' was a flushing device, but since no mention was made of a valve or trap to seal off the sewer gases it seems probable that this vital part of a true water closet was missing.

Exactly who re-introduced the idea of the valve seal is not known, though it seems to have been another Englishman. The French architect Jacques François Blondel, who illustrated valve closets in his *Maison de Plaisance* of 1738, referred to them as *'cabinets d'aisance à l'anglaise'* and clearly regarded them as an English invention. By the middle of the eighteenth century the water closet, though far from common, had become a reasonably well-known luxury. Campbell in his *A Compendious View of all Trades practised in the Cities of London and Westminster* published in 1747 stated that one of the duties of a plumber was to make 'pipes to convey water into our kitchens and Office Houses'. There can be little doubt that the water piped to the 'office houses' was required for flushing—a view reinforced by the fact that the Duke of Bedford is known to have installed four water closets at Woburn in 1748.

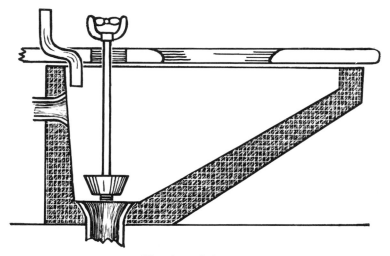

Plug closet of about 1750.

According to S. Stevens Hellyer, a nineteenth-century sanitary expert, the best type of closet available in about 1750 had the form shown in the diagram. The basin was made of marble or possibly lead, and the waste-plug was controlled by a rod extending up through the seat and ending in a handle. To flush the device the handle was pulled upwards and a cock was turned on in the service pipe. The great weakness of the design lay in the plug, for if this became worn or was not pushed firmly home it would leak and the water-seal would be lost. Some kind of subsidiary stink-trap, probably in the shape of a pot with a side tube, was at least sometimes fitted in the soil pipe itself as an additional precaution. This type of trap, however, carried risks of its own and was criticized by Cumming on the grounds that 'although it may serve effectually to cut off all communication of smell from the drains, pipe, and cesspool, it becomes in itself a magazine of foetid matter, which emits an offensive smell every time it is disturbed by using the water closet'.

Alexander Cumming was the Bond Street watchmaker who in 1775 took out the first British patent for a water closet. In his specification he was careful to avoid the older type of stink-trap, and used instead the much superior S-bend water-seal, constructed in such a way that its contents were 'totally emptied every time the closet (was) used'. This trap was perhaps the most important feature of the whole design which in other respects was no more than an ingenious adaptation of the valve closet principle. Another useful innovation, however, was the way in which a single lever was connected to the sealing valve and the water-cock, so that flushing and opening could be accomplished simultaneously. The only real weakness of the mechanism lay in the valve, which slid out sideways and must have been very difficult to keep watertight.

This deficiency was partially overcome in a patent taken out by Joseph Bramah only three years later. In this design the valve was hinged so that it could be swung down or cranked firmly into position against its seating by the operation of a lever. The drawing attached to the inventor's specification shows a string or wire running from a spur on the cranking mechanism, which strongly suggests the use of a lever-operated flush similar in principle to that employed today. An overflow pipe complete with a U-bend stink-trap was included to prevent flooding in the case of accidental leakage from the flushing device. Altogether the closet was a very workmanlike affair, and despite occasional problems with the valve won such a high reputation that over 6,000 were sold in the first twenty years of its existence. The type retained its popularity for over a century.

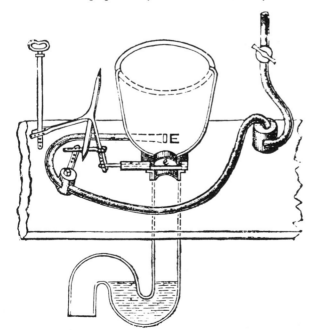

Cumming's water closet, 1775.

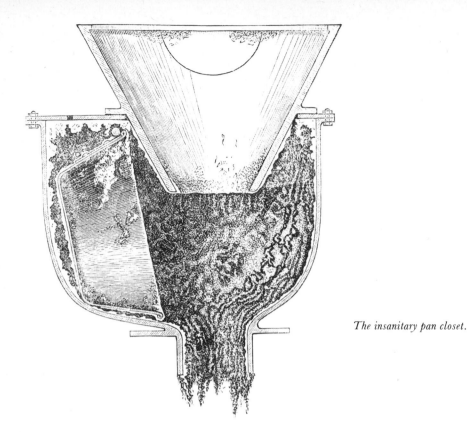

The insanitary pan closet.

Unfortunately, however, the difficulty sometimes experienced in making the valve leak-proof led to the introduction of the insanitary 'pan closet'. This device took its name from the hinged vessel which replaced the flat valve. When raised and filled with water the pan sealed off the bottom of the conical basin quite efficiently. The fault lay in the fact that a large iron container was needed to allow the pan room to swing down and empty. As the container could not readily be cleaned it became a miniature cesspit, ready to vent its gases whenever the closet was flushed. The pan closet probably originated during the 1790s, but was little used until the nineteenth century when its low price and ability to stand up to rough usage gradually brought it into vogue. At one time it was, despite its sanitary shortcomings, the most widely used of all closets. Thousands were still being exported to Russia in the early 1890s, although by then it had become thoroughly discredited in Britain.

But however good or bad a closet might be, much of its ultimate value depended on connection to an efficient drain. During the earlier part of the nineteenth century the construction of sewers lagged sadly behind the development of the water closet. Until 1815 it was forbidden for Londoners to discharge soil pipes into the capital's ramshackle rainwater sewers, and even when this was permitted, the untreated sewage was simply allowed to pour straight into the Thames in the very heart of the city. Many houses retained the cellar cesspit common since Stuart times. The euphemistically named nightmen with their buckets and carts were kept as active as ever. During the 1840s reformers like Edwin Chadwick began to alert public opinion to the truly appalling conditions in which the poor of the great cities lived. A spate of sewer construction followed, but at first much of the effort, though well intentioned, was misdirected. It was not until 1856 that London initiated work on an entirely new network of properly engineered sewers leading to an outfall situated well down-river on the Thames estuary. When finished in 1875 the 83 miles (133 km.) of main sewer could cope efficiently with 120 million gallons (545 million litres) of effluent every day. London's health record improved dramatically. A new standard for city drainage had been set.

Chadwick had recommended that all houses, even the very poorest, should be provided with water closets. As his ideas gained ground the demand for sanitary appliances increased enormously, creating a new market which many inventors and manufacturers were eager to exploit. The trade papers of the late 1840s and early 1850s are full of hopeful advertisements, extolling the virtues of this or that patent closet. From a study of these faded pages the historian can gather interesting clues to the stages by which the modern toilet evolved.

On the evidence of the advertisement columns of *The Builder* it is clear that by the late 1840s valve and pan basins were experiencing serious competition from the much cheaper 'hopper' closet, which relied simply on a water-seal to prevent the escape of sewer gases. The hopper consisted of a cone-shaped glazed-pottery bowl tapering sharply into an S-bend trap at the bottom, and provided at the top with a side-pipe for flushing water. Since there were no moving parts, cranks, or levers, the hopper could be sold at a price that even the poor could afford—seven shillings and sixpence, complete with trap, as against twenty-seven shillings for the cheapest pan closet. Unfortunately, however, the hopper suffered from one great disadvantage. The water at the bottom of the cone occupied such a small area that the exposed sides inevitably became fouled in a way which defied the feeble cleansing power of the side-injected flush. But improvements were on the way. Early in 1849 Stephen Green advertised his patent self-flushing closet which boasted, among other refinements, a much shorter basin fitted with a flushing rim of the sort later to become standard. This was a great step forward, but the shape of the basin still left much to be desired.

One simple improvement, introduced by the London-based firm of 135

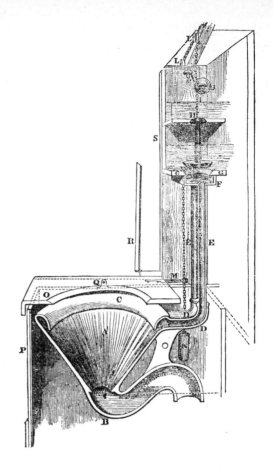

Stephen Green's self-flushing closet of 1849.

Doulton and Watts, was to angle the hopper forward so that the rear surface was vertical and less likely to be soiled. By mid-1852 the rival concern of William Northen had taken up this idea, but hardly had the changes been made when they were out-dated by further alterations of design suggested by the ingenious Stephen Green. *Green's New and Improved Closet Pan* was advertised in *The Builder* of 17 July 1852 as having 'a larger water surface than any other kind of trapped Pan, by which arrangement the sides are kept perfectly clean'. All it lacked to be almost indistinguishable from the modern wash-down toilet was the flushing rim which Green omitted though he had already used it in one of his previous models.

But the 'wash-down' closet, as so nearly perfected by Stephen Green, was not without rivals. One, announced in September 1852 by George Jennings, was an entirely new concept in water-trapped basins—the prototype of what were later to be known as 'wash-out' closets. This design featured a shallow, water-filled bowl just below the sitter and a separate water-seal lower down. Its inventor asserted that it had 'the same water surface as a

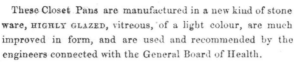

DOULTON AND WATTS'S

REGISTERED CLOSET PANS IN

ENAMELLED STONE WARE,

LAMBETH POTTERY, LONDON.

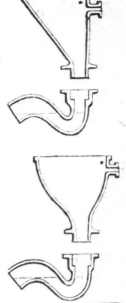

These Closet Pans are manufactured in a new kind of stone ware, HIGHLY GLAZED, vitreous, of a light colour, are much improved in form, and are used and recommended by the engineers connected with the General Board of Health.

The Traps are smaller at the inlet, gradually enlarging towards the outlet, as a security against the introduction of improper substances into the drain.

They may also be had turned down.

PRICE 7s. 6d. EACH,

The same as for ordinary stone ware, and may be had fitted with copper fans of the best construction at 1s. 3d. each extra.

Doulton and Watts' improved hopper closets, 1852.

THE BUILDER.

NEW AND IMPROVED CLOSET PANS.

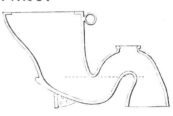

STEPHEN GREEN AND CO.

IMPERIAL POTTERIES, LAMBETH.

These Pans will be found to combine all the latest improvements, with the advantage of having a larger water surface than any other kind of trapped Pan, by which arrangement the sides are kept perfectly clean. The trap is not larger than usual, and has its smallest diameter at the bottom of the Pan, increasing to the end so that anything passing the neck cannot possibly stop or clog the drain.

Manufactured in superior double-glazed Stoneware, white and smooth inside, at the SAME PRICE AS THE COMMON PAN; with Patent Valve, 1s. 6d extra.

MANUFACTURERS OF THE PATENT SYPHON FLUSHING-BASIN, AND IMPROVED DRAIN PIPES.

Green's New and Improved Closet Pan *as advertised in* The Builder *of 17 July 1852.*

valve closet, and all the advantages of pan or other closets without any disadvantages, as it displaces no impure air'. Alongside Jennings' powerful challenge, the older types of closet continue to vie for a share in the market. The expense of valve closets seems to have blessed them with a curious snob appeal, which for long ensured their popularity with the upper class. Hoppers survived for the very opposite reason; their low cost made many willing to forgive their faults.

So matters rested for several decades. The public had a wide choice of 137

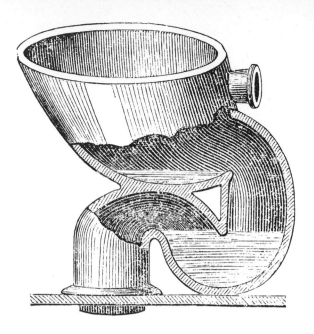

*Jennings' wash-out closet
announced in 1852 represented a
blind alley in the development of
the modern toilet.*

closets at its disposal, and it was only very slowly that the wash-down and
the wash-out emerged as the most favoured types. As late as 1877 S. Steven
Hellyer, in his book *The Plumber and Sanitary Houses*, found it necessary to
warn householders of the shortcomings of the old-fashioned hopper, evidently
still much in use. Then, going on to speak of the more advanced water-trap
closets, he conceded that the wash-out variety was 'much liked by some
people', but made it quite clear that his own preference lay with the wash-
down. Hellyer's judgement has been vindicated by the almost universal
acceptance of this type of closet during the twentieth century.

But the appearance of toilets was still not as it is today. Most closets were
boxed in, partly for the look of the thing and partly to give structural
support to the seat. There were exceptions. An advertisement in *The Builder*
of 21 April 1849 for the *Torrent* water closet shows an obviously free-standing
model which, it is stated, 'can be encased in wood, and rendered as handsome in appearance as any other'. However, it is generally accepted that
the 'pedestal' closet, designed specifically so as to require no unhygienic
surround, did not appear and achieve popularity until the 1880s.

There seem to be two contenders for the honour of having introduced
this final improvement. Joseph Hatton, in his book *Twyfords* written in
1905, recorded that in the summer of 1885 this famous firm of potters was
approached by 'a French architect of advanced views in sanitary engineering, who desired to know if he could be supplied with a basin to be fixed
open and exposed, without any wooden enclosure. Mr. Twyford replied in

the affirmative, and had at once a design prepared and submitted to the architect, who was so pleased with it that 700 were at once ordered . . .' Twyford's pedestal was, however, of the now obsolete wash-out form, so perhaps greater credit should go to Frederick Humpherson who brought out his free-standing *Beaufort* wash-down in the same year. This closet gained the Certificate of Merit of the Sanitary Institute of Great Britain, and set the pattern for the future.

Although the pedestal wash-down is now the type most generally used in advanced countries throughout the world, the siphonic closet is also favoured for its almost silent action. There are many varieties of this class, but all have the exit pipe so shaped that it can sustain a siphoning action to remove the contents of the bowl. The violent and noisy flush associated with the wash-down closet is not required.

The siphonic idea was introduced by John Randall Mann in 1870 and although his original design, with its three separate delivery pipes for water, was itself too complex to secure wide acceptance, it acted as a stimulus to

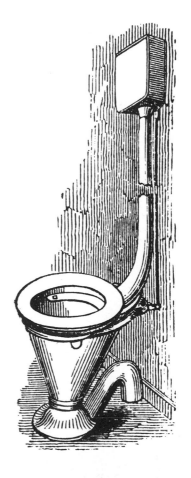

The Torrent *water closet, a free-standing design from 1849.*

other inventors. Within six years William Smith had patented a siphonic closet in the United States—the first of many to appear in that country. Development also continued in Britain. Twyfords were marketing their siphonic *Twycliffe* in 1894, and by 1896 the Scottish firm of Shanks were claiming that their *Barrhead* was free from all the problems previously associated with closets working on the siphon principle.

Wash-down and siphonic closets have stood the test of time remarkably well. Despite inevitable alterations in styling they have remained unchanged in essentials since the turn of the century. As water-carriage sanitation has spread gradually across the world, the water closet has followed—one of Britain's great contributions to civilized living.

It is only recently that the water closet's single major weakness, its thirst for water, has begun to cause concern. Each flush of a standard cistern uses two gallons (9·1 litres). In arid regions this is a serious problem, and even in countries with temperate climates increasing populations are putting a serious strain on water resources. One way of reducing demand has been

Page from the 1899 Twyfords catalogue.

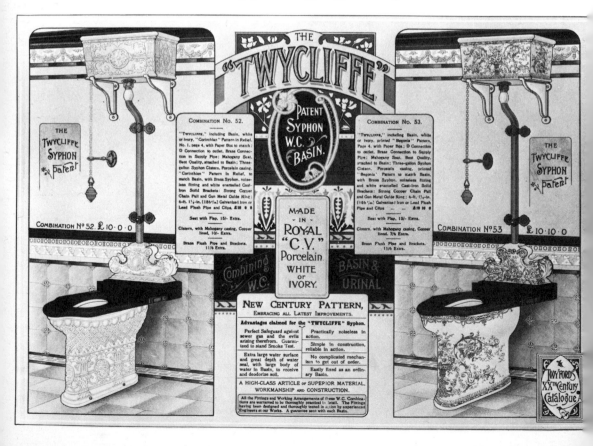

suggested with the 'Dual Flushing Cistern' which can deliver a one-gallon flush when the full quantity is not required. A much more radical solution has come from the Swedish engineer Joel Lilljendahl, who has invented the entirely new 'vacuum' water closet. This device employs a small pump to reduce the pressure in the soil pipe so that the contents of the basin are positively sucked out and only a tiny cleansing flush of about one-eighth the usual amount is required. The comparatively small amount of soiled water is collected in a special tank from which it can be piped to a local chemical treatment plant. Apart from the question of cost the appeal of the system for those living away from main drainage or in dry, tropical areas is obvious. Vacuum closets have been used in Sweden itself since 1959 and have also been installed in Mexico City and the Bahamas. Their large-scale adoption in developed countries with adequate conventional sewerage is, however, doubtful. The pre-eminence of the traditional closet seems secure for the foreseeable future.

7

Making a House a Home

A deserted house bereft of all furnishings is strangely disturbing and hostile
—a place of echoing memories, not quite dead but drained of vitality. Only
when its bare walls and floors are re-clothed with the possessions of new
owners does it spring back to life and friendliness. Furniture and decorations
give a house individuality and help to make it into a home.

Probably man has always felt the need to impress his personality on whatever dwelling-place he might occupy. Neanderthal people are known to
have buried well-loved relatives in masses of blossom; is it too much to
suspect that they might have decorated the abodes of the living in the same
way? Furnishings must, however, have remained extremely makeshift and
transitory until the spread of agriculture enabled men to establish permanent
settlements and long-lasting houses.

The earth-covered mound of Çatal Hüyük in Turkey hides the ruins of
a remarkable town built by an agricultural people 8,000 years ago. Here
are to be found not only some of the earliest houses yet discovered but
indications of how they were furnished and decorated. Most families had
two rectangular rooms—one for living and the other for storage purposes.
The layout of the living-room seems to have been dictated by ancient
custom, for there are striking similarities in the arrangements of many
different dwellings. A low, mud-brick platform, usually divided into two
parts, ran for most of the length of the eastern wall before terminating in
a slightly higher position at the southern end. This was the furniture of the
house, serving as bed during the night and bench during the day. It is
thought that the smaller part of the platform, in the corner of the room, was
reserved for the male head of the household while the remaining space was
shared by the women and children.

Although the accommodation was rather austere, there were relieving
touches of unexpected luxury. Some walls were decorated with designs or
pictures—the earliest known paintings on man-made structures. Most of
the paintings were religious in nature and occurred in what were obviously

special rooms set aside as shrines, but a few were secular. Amongst this latter group were designs imitating textile patterns of the sort used in carpet making. It seems clear that the people of Çatal Hüyük had already mastered the complicated art of weaving, and quite probably decorated their houses with brightly coloured mats.

The houses of other early agriculturalists also contain surprises. Not only were the wattle-and-daub dwellings of the fourth millennium B.C. farmers of the Bulgarian plain painted in brilliant colours within and without, but, on the evidence of clay models, they were further graced by furniture of considerable sophistication. From actual house remains it is known that a favourite decorative scheme for internal walls was alternate horizontal stripes of maroon and white with a superimposed pattern of oval shapes and linking curves. No actual furniture has survived from this period, but the models are enough to show that the carpentry of these ancient farmers more than matched the bold vigour of their murals. Reproduced in clay are elegant wooden-framed chairs with padded seats and benches resembling modern settees.

Such a life-style could only be maintained under favourable conditions, and few other prehistoric cultures could have approached such a level of home comfort. Nevertheless man can adapt to the most uncompromising

Model furniture from ancient settlements in Bulgaria, fourth millennium B.C.

Interior of a house at Skara Brae, the remarkable Neolithic settlement founded on Mainland Orkney late in the third millennium B.C.

of environments. The windswept Orkneys, too cold for cereal crops and devoid of trees, could still produce in the late third millennium B.C. the remarkable settlement of Skara Brae, whose inhabitants seem to have lived mainly by cattle-raising. To give some protection from the weather the stone-built houses had to be half-buried in the earth, but inside they were snug enough. All the furniture was built-in, and to overcome the lack of wood, constructed from broken pieces of the abundant local flagstone. Bed-nooks were arranged on either side of the central fireplace and isolated from the rest of the room by large vertical slabs. Opposite the entrance was a sort of dresser with stone shelves supported on bearer walls. The people of Skara Brae made such good use of their meagre resources that their ruined houses still seem welcoming and homelike.

The great civilizations of Mesopotamia and Egypt arose in much more favoured regions, but they too were poor in wood. Mud and reeds, however, were to be had in plenty, and it was to these that the poorer people turned for the materials needed to construct their homes. The mud-brick houses they built were furnished with mud-brick couches and benches, while the floors were covered by mats woven from the ever-present reeds.

Much more detailed information is available about the contents of wealthy households. In Egypt this comes not only from wall paintings, reliefs, and statues, but from the traditional practice of burying dead nobles and officials surrounded by all the comforts they had enjoyed in life. The dry Egyptian climate favours preservation, and a large selection of ancient furniture has survived, some of it virtually intact, down to the present day. Little, however, has been found in the tombs of the Old and Middle Kingdoms (third and early second millennium B.C.) except fragments of beds consisting of raised wooden frames covered with animal hides. It seems that even the wealthy of those remote times were usually content to squat during the day on mats or cushions spread on the floor.

Stools and chairs were, of course, not completely unknown in ancient Egypt. Even before the first great Pharaoh united the whole country under his rule the peasantry were making stools from papyrus and bent wood. On the evidence of artwork, chairs, too, may be traced back to the early days of Pharaonic Egypt, but it is clear that they were always thought of more as thrones than ordinary articles of furniture. The noble sat on a chair to receive the homage of his subjects; at ease with friends he lolled upon cushions.

With the advent of the New Kingdom (1555–712 B.C.) finds of furniture

An ancient Egyptian wall-painting showing interior and fittings of a house.

This impression from a Sumerian cylinder seal of the third millennium B.C. shows the simplicity of the furniture used by even the most important of people.

become richer. The tomb of one high official and his wife contained, for instance, two beds with wooden headrests, a dozen stools, several stands, many boxes and storage chests, but, significantly, only one chair. Though more furniture was in use, the chair was still something of a ceremonial object and the household interior remained functional and uncluttered. Great use was made of mats, both on the floor and as decorative hangings on the walls.

Because conditions in Mesopotamia do not favour the preservation of wood no really ancient pieces of furniture, apart from a few mud-brick benches, have come down to us from this region. Instead reliance must be placed on surviving works of art, which, since they were made for the wealthy and reflect their interests, give a rather lopsided picture of Mesopotamian civilization. The reliefs, the statues, and the imprints left by cylinder seals depict the great and their doings rather than the simple home-life of ordinary people.

On the pictorial evidence available, however, it would seem that even the palaces of early Mesopotamia held little in the way of furniture. Chairs with backs and occasionally arms were known, but it is clear from the reliefs in which they appeared that they were only used when the sitter wished to emphasize his dignity and rank. For less formal occasions the mightiest of kings did not despise the humble comfort of a backless stool. Feast scenes inscribed on cylinder seals made during the first half of the third millennium

B.C. sometimes show royal or perhaps divine revellers perched on stools around a communal wine jar into which each has dipped a drinking tube. The only other piece of furniture to be illustrated on ancient Mesopotamian seals was a rather tall flat-topped stand—possibly a dining table, but, because of its height, much more probably a type of sideboard from which food could be served to the diners.

In the early days of the Mesopotamian civilization to have any furniture more elaborate than the simplest stool or mud-brick couch was a sign of wealth and nobility. Gradually, however, lower members of society began to aspire to a higher standard of living.

Although no trace remains of the movables which once graced the middle-class homes of second-millennium Ur, the spaciousness of the excavated house-shells suggests a considerable degree of comfort. A family wealthy enough to afford such a house, with its two storeys and upwards of a dozen rooms, would hardly have baulked at the expense of a few stools, table-stands, and perhaps even chairs. The upstairs rooms would have contained raised wooden-framed beds and possibly one or two storage chests for the family's clothing and valuables. Mats and cushions would have been strewn in profusion about the house to provide the bulk of the seating. The rooms themselves were tall, as befitted such a hot climate, and the general impression of airiness must have been reinforced by the whitewash applied to the carefully plastered walls.

During the earlier half of the first millennium B.C., Mesopotamia was engulfed by the Assyrian Empire. Cities and provinces were overrun and their goods carried off by the victors. By this time kings had long outgrown their ancient austerity, and luxury furniture from their palaces figured largely in the booty. One list, compiled in the ninth century B.C., mentions tables of costly wood and couches of ivory overlaid with gold looted from the residence of a defeated prince. The existence of such couches, surely too ornate to be mere beds, suggests that the custom of reclining at meals had

Relief showing King Ashurbanipal of Assyria (668–631 B.C.) at dinner.

Greek vase-painting showing a dining couch.

already become established. Certainly the later Assyrian monarchs preferred this somewhat uncomfortable mode of dining. A relief has survived which shows King Ashurbanipal (668–631 B.C.) stretched out on a high couch, enjoying a meal in the company of his wife, who, more sensibly, is seated upon a chair.

The fashion for horizontal dining spread to classical Greece, where the couch became the most important item of furniture in the middle-class home. No self-respecting household could do without enough couches for at least a dozen guests, but this was neither so extravagant nor space-consuming as might be imagined. Each couch was big enough to accommodate up to three people, while at night it could double as a bed. The Greek couch was basically a very simple piece of furniture—light enough to be moved by a single servant. Its mattress was supported on cords strung between the sides of a rectangular wooden frame, which was held well clear of the ground on four tapering legs. Often the legs at one end were made an inch or two longer than those at the other so that the couch sloped slightly upwards towards the head. Striped cushions were piled at the higher end to support the diner as he reclined at his meal. Each couch was provided with a low, three- or four-legged table on which food or drinks could be stood. When not in use the table was tucked away beneath its couch.

Apart from the dining-room, Greek homes were sparsely furnished. There might be a few chairs with padded seats and a scattering of stools, perhaps with legs modelled on those of animals, but there would be no cupboards or wardrobes. Everyday possessions were hung from hooks on the wall, while items too precious or bulky for such treatment were stowed in wooden chests.

In the Roman world the couch retained the popularity which it had enjoyed among the Greeks. Rich houses possessed elaborate dining couches, sometimes cast in bronze and often draped in costly fabrics. The Emperor Nero actually spent the equivalent of £50,000 just to provide new covers for his banqueting suite. Even humble homes owned couches of a sort, though these were no more than brick wall-shelves, which could serve as seats by day and beds by night.

The poorer sort of Roman, who usually lived in a tall tenement building, had very few possessions to cheer his home. According to the satirist, Juvenal, such a person could sweep all his goods into a single bundle, should he need to flee from one of the devastating fires which frequently ravaged the city. What these meagre 'bits and pieces' would have been must remain guesswork since no classical author thought it worth his while to describe the furnishings of a plebeian flat. Probably, however, the bundle would have held bedding, spare clothes, a brazier for cooking and heating, a few knives and spoons, pots, platters, and cups, a couple of cheap lamps, and little more.

Even rich homes were sparsely furnished by modern standards. Romans preferred to show their wealth by the quality rather than the profusion of their goods. Apart from couches, the dining-room, for instance, would have contained only a table and perhaps a tiered buffet for the display of silver. The table, however, might be of such rare workmanship that it was excessively costly. Seneca, a leading statesman of Nero's reign, paid £35,000 for one superb specimen, beautifully inlaid with precious woods.

Other rooms were equally uncluttered. In the private family apartments there would be a few stools and benches for the men, chairs for the women, and of course those indispensable couches on which the Romans liked to loll, even when they were reading or writing. Bedrooms were particularly stark. They seldom contained more than a single chair or stool, a chest, a chamber pot, and the bed itself. The only concession to luxury was the mat that covered the floor. With plenty of slave labour available, all the rooms were kept clean and tidy. Household possessions not required for the moment were stored out of sight, sometimes in chests but increasingly in the built-in cupboards and wardrobes, which had by now come into widespread use. Walls were no longer defaced by hooks and all manner of suspended belongings as they had been in Greek times.

But if rooms were rather bare of furniture, those intended for day-time use were very far from austere. Walls were a riot of colour, setting off the statues of marble and bronze that were common in all wealthy homes. Several modes of decoration were employed. Some walls were hung with gorgeous tapestries; others were covered with painted or mosaic panels. All manner of scenes were depicted, ranging from legendary episodes to still-life renderings of fish and other marine creatures. No subject seemed too grand nor too humble. In the more important rooms at least, the richness of the walls was matched by the splendour of a mosaic pavement. Floor designs were, if anything, even more intricate than those featured on walls, though the colours were usually more subdued. Sometimes patterns were cleverly contrived to give startling optical effects which must have been very disturbing for unwary or slightly tipsy guests. Ceilings also were not neglected, but were painted in strong, bright colours.

This fashion for vivid decoration, so suited to the sunshine of the Mediterranean, spread throughout the Roman world, finding favour even in misty Britain. Wealthy colonists and Romanized natives copied the style, and many of the mosaic pavements with which they embellished their villas have survived down to the present day.

The wealthy Roman often decorated the floors of his house with elaborate mosaics.

But in many provinces Roman civilization could have been little more than a veneer superimposed on a substratum of unchanging tribal customs. Although Roman-style houses dotted the landscape in many fertile regions, the bulk of the population preferred to live in native villages. The imported culture had not succeeded in sinking deep roots. When the military power of the Western Empire crumbled in the fifth and sixth centuries and the security which had made villa-life possible gave way to anarchy, all pretence at sophistication was quickly lost. With the disappearance of the villa, European domestic comfort suffered a setback from which it was not to recover until the nineteenth century.

The Anglo-Saxon invaders of Britain had no taste for Roman elegance. To them the ideal home for a chieftain was a barn-like structure flanked by a few outhouses. The main building served as a hall in which the leader's henchmen ate, drank, and slept. There was little furniture, and what there was had to be set close to the wall as the centre of the room was taken up by a huge fireplace. Tables were mere boards laid over trestles so that they could be stacked away once a meal was over. The simple benches on which the diners sat had to serve as beds at night. Only the lord and the more honoured of his guests withdrew to the comparative luxury of beds made up in one or other of the outhouses. Even here, however, the standard of comfort left a lot to be desired, since the bed provided was probably nothing more than a straw-filled mattress resting in a shallow wooden box held just clear of the ground on short, clumsy legs.

Peasants lived in wretched conditions, and their wattle-and-daub huts usually lacked any furniture. Rough seats would have been contrived from whatever materials came to hand; a pile of straw would have sufficed for a bed. The most important domestic possessions would have been the housewife's cooking pots.

In England the Norman Conquest displaced the old Saxon nobility, but although it subjected the peasantry to a sterner form of feudalism it left their home-life little affected for better or for worse. Taxation records compiled for the country town of Colchester reveal that as late as 1301 most of the inhabitants had no household possessions of sufficient value to warrant a mention. It was not until later in the fourteenth century that the ordinary people began to benefit from a gradual advance in domestic comfort. But just how slowly things improved may be judged from William Harrison's assertion, contained in a book written in 1577, that men of his grandfather's generation had been accustomed to sleep on 'straw pallets or rough mats'. Conditions seem to have been little better even in the advanced Netherlands, for the work of such sixteenth-century artists as

The furniture used by ordinary people remained rough and ready for long after the medieval period had passed. This drawing, taken from a contemporary painting of a seventeenth-century Dutch alehouse, shows just how crude the furniture could be.

Pieter Bruegel contain ample evidence of the simplicity of contemporary peasant furniture.

Noble households made faster progress, but for long there was more grandeur than real comfort. Medieval magnates often possessed several widely separated estates, and travelled backwards and forwards between them—never staying for long in any one. There was little incentive to spend money on fitting out dwellings which were left unused for much of the year. As a result furniture was kept to the minimum and what there was tended to be crudely made except for a few portable items. Lords often possessed finely decorated folding stools which accompanied them on their journeys. Their halls, however, were furnished with the simplest of trestle tables and benches. Bedchambers were almost equally utilitarian. Alexander Neckham, writing about 1180, described, as his ideal, a room where the bed had a chair at its side and a bench at its foot. Projecting from the wall should be two poles—one to act as clothes hanger, the other as perch for the falcons.

The only concession to luxury would be provided by the hangings which hid the cold bareness of the walls. Since Neckham was Richard the Lion Heart's foster brother and moved much in court circles, it may be assumed that his description represents the ultimate in twelfth-century comfort.

In the East carpets had been used to decorate walls from time immemorial, and it is possible that the European fashion for rich hangings received an impetus from the experience of the Crusades. Western warriors could not but have been impressed by the superiority of Arab culture, and what novelty more calculated to appeal to a lord of many estates than a gorgeous wall-covering that could be rolled up and transported to whichever of his several homes he intended to visit? Here was elegance on the cheap. It soon became customary to drape not only the walls but also furniture. Benches and chairs had embroidered materials thrown over them, while beds were provided with curtains—initially suspended from iron rods driven into the wall but from the fourteenth century sometimes supported by a frame attached to the bed itself. Hangings were not, however, the only wall decoration. Plaster and paint were relatively cheap, and were frequently used to add a touch of gaiety to the sombre grey stones of the medieval fortress. Sometimes simple patterns were employed—Henry III, who reigned from 1216 to 1272, particularly favoured a design of gold stars painted on a plain green background. Others preferred their walls to tell a story, and covered them with scenes from the bible or some well-known romance. The thirteenth-century lay of Sir Guinivere spoke, for instance, of a room 'from roof to

Private chamber in a twelfth-century French chateau.

Private chamber in a thirteenth-century French chateau.

floor with golden imageries pictured o'er', while a poem of a hundred years later contained the description of

> 'A chamber paint
> Full of stories old and divers'.

Yet another way of giving a room a homely look was to line it with wooden boards, which were themselves often painted. Wainscoting, as this panelling process was called, was certainly being practised during the thirteenth century, though it did not become really popular until Tudor times.

Floors seem to have received less attention than walls. In the nobleman's hall it long remained the custom to take off the chill of the pavement with a covering of rushes or straw, and as late as the reign of Elizabeth I the public rooms of Greenwich Palace were strewn with bay leaves. Private rooms, of course, received more luxurious treatment from a far earlier date. The thirteenth-century Austrian poet Ulrich von Lichtenstein could boast in his 'Frauendienst' that the floor of his lady's chamber could not be seen for the many fair carpets. Bedroom rugs are said to have been introduced to England from Moorish Spain during the kingship of Edward I (1272–1307).

As the Middle Ages drew to a close in the fifteenth century, government became more centralized and the high nobility found less necessity to move from house to house in pursuit of the court. Now there was more incentive to spend money on the furnishings of a favourite residence. By this time also the successful town-merchant had emerged, with only one house to bother about, and the wealth and inclination to make it the envy of his neighbours. Gradually the improvements in domestic comfort, so encouraged, spread downwards to even the humbler levels of society. Writing towards the end of the sixteenth century, William Harrison was able to claim that:

> 'The furniture of our houses also exceedeth and is grown in a manner even to passing delicacy; and here I do not speak of the nobility and gentry only but like-wise of the lowest sort. . . .'

Harrison's words, however, must be taken with a pinch of salt. There were undoubtedly more rooms in all kinds of houses, except the poorest, and these extra rooms had somehow to be filled, but furniture remained far from plentiful. The hall, which by now was rapidly declining in import-ance, had only its long tables and benches and little else but a couple of chairs and a few cupboards to relieve its bareness. In great houses hall tables were usually solid and enormous, but in farmhouses and cottages collapsible trestle tables retained their old popularity. As the first-floor gallery gradually took over as the principal room in fashionable homes, furniture styles altered. The massive box chair with its solid wooden back and arm-rests and its built-in cupboard under the seat was all very well when intended to stand immovable in the master's place at top table in the

Private chamber in a fifteenth-century French chateau. Notice the increased luxury compared with the rooms in the previous two illustrations.

A reconstruction of Ockwells, Berkshire, showing the wainscoting and simple furniture of a fifteenth-century hall.

hall, but it was not suited to an upper room. Lighter chairs that could be moved relatively easily appeared. Some were based on the box-design but with legs replacing the heavy cupboard; others were developed from the ancient folding-stool and had legs crossing to form an X-shape. The very rich even began to indulge in the unheard of luxury of upholstered chairs.

Although chairs were coming into more common use, it was still customary for only the more important personages in a gathering to be provided with them. Queen Elizabeth might sit on her cushioned chair, but around her the courtiers perched uncomfortably on hard stools or benches. The same veneration for the chair was observed in private homes. It was unusual for a room to contain more than one or two of them. The master and perhaps the mistress might sit enthroned; the rest of the family made do with stools and forms or improvised seats from storage chests.

Chests were still widely used, especially for blankets and linen, but the various cupboards which had developed from the hutch or doored-chest during the later Middle Ages were much more in evidence than before. The chest was also evolving in another direction. Towards the end of the sixteenth century it occurred to some unknown craftsmen that it would be more sensible to make the box shallower and fit a drawer beneath it. Perhaps his wife had been grumbling at having to rummage through the entire contents of a chest to get to some article at the bottom. Over the next hundred years the box portion was made progressively smaller until in the end it was often omitted altogether. The familiar chest of drawers had been born.

Before the sixteenth century ordinary people had often slept on the floor, but as the bedchamber became more common, so did proper beds. Cottages did not, of course, possess the enormous four-posters complete with wooden canopies and costly curtains that graced the mansions of the wealthy.

A fifteenth-century box chair.

The drawing-room in Haddon Hall, Derbyshire, as it might have appeared early in the seventeenth century.

Instead they had simple bedsteads perhaps consisting of little more than a straw pallet lying on plain wooden boards, though Harrison does maintain that feather-beds were beginning to find their way into the houses of at least the more prosperous of yeomen.

In the matter of interior decoration, the sixteenth century produced little that was positively new. The increasing size of windows did encourage a freer use of stained glass in the domestic setting, but, as Harrison makes quite clear, the treatment of walls remained strictly traditional. 'The walls of our houses,' he wrote, 'be either hanged with tapestries or Arras work or painted clothes, wherein either divers histories or herbs, or beasts, knots and such like are stained; or else they are ceiled with oak of our own, or wainscote brought out of the east countries. . . .' He makes no mention of wallpaper, so although some is known to have been produced as early as 1509, it must have failed to catch on and been quickly forgotten. One innovation, however, which exerted a powerful influence on contemporary taste was the introduction into Britain of the Italian technique of decorating ceilings with plaster mouldings.

During the seventeenth century both the house and its contents began to take on a distinctly modern aspect. The hall, for instance, continued its steady decline in size and importance, so that by Queen Anne's reign it had degenerated into a mere vestibule, providing access to the groundfloor rooms and the staircase. Furniture of all sorts was more common. In most families, except the poorest, there were now chairs for everyone, and, although hard seats still predominated, upholstery was no longer the pre-rogative of the exceptionally rich. This was the age in which the settee appeared—an elegant and cushioned descendant of the old-fashioned settle. Chests continued to linger on in cottages, but in better-off homes cupboards were the vogue. There were separate cupboards for food, linen, and clothes; there were bookcases with glazed doors; there were even glass-fronted cabinets in which china could be displayed. By the end of the century the chest of drawers had also achieved widespread acceptance.

Not only was there more furniture, but its appearance was improved. The heavy, bulbous look of the sixteenth century gradually gave way to slimmer, more pleasing lines. After about 1660, for example, the massive oak dining table lost favour, and was supplanted by lighter variants, often oval in shape and provided with gate-legs to allow a flap to be folded down when not required. Oak was much less used than formerly, being increasingly replaced by walnut in more expensive items. Veneers and inlays of coloured wood began to assume an important decorative role. In keeping with these general trends ornately carved bed-heads and monumental bed-posts dropped in esteem. Bed-curtains, however, retained all their old popularity, and those who could afford to do so continued to lavish much money upon them.

Interior decoration generally followed along well-established lines. Wall-hangings remained much in demand, though leather had begun to replace embroidered fabric in popular regard. Samuel Pepys records, in his diary entry for 19 October 1660, that his dining-room had just been 'finished with green serge hangings and gilt leather, which is very handsome'. The old practice of painting designs directly on wall surfaces also continued, but wainscoting had by now emerged as easily the most favoured of wall treatments. The fashion for decorating ceilings with elaborate plaster mouldings flourished unabated. Floors, on the other hand, were usually constructed of plain boards of polished oak, wide spaces of which were left uncovered in even the best of homes, despite the increasing use of carpets. Cottagers bought cheap plaited-rush mats to hide their bare boards. The habit of scattering loose rushes on the floor had by now almost completely died out, even in country districts.

Although methods of room decoration had remained largely traditional, 159

An interior from a middle-class home, late eighteenth century.

a major change was on the way. After a long gap, since its first hesitating introduction, wallpaper came back and gradually gained acceptance. It seems likely that flock paperhangings, giving an appearance of velvet, were in small-scale production in France by about 1630, but at such an early date paper was certainly regarded as a second best for people whose means did not stretch to fabrics or leather. This attitude began to alter after the introduction of Chinese wallpaper into Europe at about mid-century. A craze for eastern fashions was already taking hold, so imported papers acquired a snob appeal. Local production was considerably encouraged and by 1699 John Houghton, a Fellow of the Royal Society, could write that 'a great deal of Paper is nowadays printed to be pasted upon Walls to serve instead of hangings; and truly if all Parts of the Sheet be well and close pasted on, it is very pritty, clean and will last with tolerable Care a great while. . . .'

But despite Houghton's brave words, wallpaper was still in its infancy, and another forty years of uphill work were required before it really established itself. As late as 1756 an English visitor to Holland noted that the Dutch had 'not come into the taste of paper in their houses; velvet and leather hangings still being much used'. By mid-eighteenth century wainscoting was gradually falling from favour, but its place was as often taken by stucco reliefs as wallpaper. The stucco treatment, with flat areas painted in soft colours and the raised portions picked out in white or gold was particularly suited to the proportions of large houses, where it continued in use into the nineteenth century. Wallpaper, however, was triumphing with the middle classes. The price barrier to its even wider employment was finally removed with the advent of cheap, machine-made papers in the early 1840s. Since that date it has been one of the decorator's chief standbys, in rich and poor houses alike.

While these alterations were taking place in the way in which rooms were decorated, the contents were also changing. France was the powerhouse of innovation, though English influence was also considerable. Furniture styles changed only slowly during the first two or three decades of the eighteenth century, but thereafter fashion followed fashion in quick succession.

One of the dominant themes of the age was the exuberant rococo style which emerged in France in about 1735 and dominated much of the European scene until the 1760s. Rococo furniture was distinguished by its lack of symmetry and by the flowing lines of the florid carvings with which it was decorated.

In England the prevailing fashion at this time was for the so-called Palladian furniture which since it drew its inspiration from the rectilinear symmetry of Italian renaissance architecture was the very antithesis of rococo. But the wind of change was blowing hard from France. By the 1740s the rococo style had obtained a foothold and within a decade was well established in Britain. Thomas Chippendale's famous *Gentleman and Cabinet-Maker's Director*, published in 1754, contained a large range of rococo designs.

The counter-attack against the excesses of rococo decoration was spearheaded in Britain by the architect Robert Adam. He, and men like him who had travelled in Italy, were inspired anew by a love for the simplicity of classical and renaissance architecture. The furniture favoured by this new school of thought was based on symmetry and the straight line, while the classical motifs used for decoration were applied with dignity and restraint. During the 1760s Adam built up a reputation as a man who could design 161

This sketch by Thomas Rowlandson gives some idea of the neo-classical furniture designs favoured in Regency England.

not only a house but also the furniture to go with it. Though his clients were, of course, confined to the wealthier class, his ideas were taken up by a far wider circle. Furniture in the neoclassical vein was soon being made for people in the middle income-brackets.

During the first decades of the nineteenth century the fashions of Imperial France exercised a powerful influence on European taste. The Empire style, based at least partially on a study of the furniture of ancient Greece and Rome, became all the rage. Chairs and couches in particular were designed to imitate the lines of classical models, while tables were often mounted, after the Roman fashion, on legs carved to represent fantastic winged lions and the like. For pieces with no ancient precedents, designers relied on the use of straight lines and the appropriate choice of ornamentation to produce a classical effect. After about 1820 the Empire or, as the English called it, Regency style began to degenerate—its elegance giving way to heaviness and over-ostentation. At about the same time discerning observers noted an increasing tendency to cram rooms with too much furniture. The stage was being set for Victoria's reign.

It was unfortunate that this decline in taste should have been followed during the 1840s by an increasing use of machinery in furniture production. The adoption of factory methods would inevitably have resulted in some lowering of standards while new techniques were mastered, but at least the effect might have been minimized under the influence of a confident tradition of design. As it was the principal market for the factory-made furniture was provided by a new middle class thrown up by the Industrial Revolution and still so uncertain of its taste that it could only hark back to half understood themes from the past. The furniture produced by the first industrial age was a bizarre mixture of old-fashioned styles. Some pieces retained a Regency flavour; others were floridly rococo. There was even a flourishing trade in what was called 'Elizabethan' furniture, though any resemblance to the real thing was strictly coincidental.

After 1850 the choice of furniture styles was less restricted, but inspiration was generally still sought from the past. It seemed that much of the inventive vigour of the people had been exhausted during the upheaval of industrialization, so that little was left for the creation of genuinely new fashions in furniture. But although much design was clumsily repetitive, one or two ideas, more in keeping with the advance of technology, did emerge. Brass and iron tubing came into vogue for bed-heads, while the old rope-mesh support for the mattress was increasingly replaced by a grid of thick metal wires attached to an iron frame. Coiled upholstery springs, first tentatively used in the eighteenth century, were also perfected, enabling the development of much more comfortable seating. Armchairs and sofas became corpulent under heavy rolls of sprung upholstery.

Besides lowering the quality of workmanship, factory production, by

A Victorian interior. Many rooms were even more crowded.

A modern interior.

reducing the price of furniture, contributed to one of the worst features of the Victorian interior—its overcrowding. The elegant spaciousness of the previous century had given way to clutter. Material possessions seemed everything, and the more the better. In the typical middle-class drawing-room a profusion of chairs, tables, stools, flowerstands, and cabinets jostled with the piano for floor space, while the heavily patterned paper on the walls heightened the already claustrophobic effect. Even the mantelshelf was crowded—the inevitable clock being flanked with all manner of bric-à-brac and ornaments.

But the nineteenth century was not without its own critics. One of the most influential was the British designer William Morris (1834–96). Morris was so repelled by the shoddiness of machine-made furniture that he turned his back on the modern world and looked to medieval times for his inspiration. Craftsmanship was to him all-important, and this, he thought, could be achieved only by handwork based on traditional methods. His insistence on quality had a salutary effect, but his impact on popular taste would have been much greater if he had accepted the machine and attempted to improve its products.

The Werkbund, an association of German manufacturers, artists, and architects formed in 1907, had a more realistic approach. Its members followed Morris in a demand for better quality, but were not hostile to the use of machinery. Their message was that the machine was an elaborate tool that had to be mastered rather than avoided. Following in the footsteps of the Werkbund, the British Design and Industries Association was instituted in 1915, with the aim of improving the products of industry.

Still more influential in the development of new ideas in furniture design was the German Bauhaus, founded in 1919 with Walter Gropius at its head. This school trained architects, painters, and master craftsmen, and was dedicated to bringing together the different strands of creative endeavour in order to improve the standard of industrial design. From its furniture workshop issued a succession of startling new forms—tubular metal chairs, gleaming in chromium, and carefully contrived units which could be combined in numerous different ways. All non-essentials were pared away; form was made subservient to function. By the time the Nazis closed the Bauhaus in 1933 it had established a severely modern style based on hard lines and the use of metal tubing and plywood.

This unadorned style has persisted to the present, though the angularity of its lines has gradually softened. New materials have entered the scene— synthetic rubber foam for upholstery, plastic and fibreglass for moulded chair seats, coloured plastic laminates for surfaces, synthetic fibres for covers. Floor and wall-coverings have not escaped the technologists' attention. Vinyl tiles and sheeting have proved useful on kitchen and bathroom floors, while nylon has provided a much needed alternative to natural fibres in carpet manufacture. Wallpaper has been partially superseded by hard-wearing, washable vinyl. The modern home is colourful, streamlined, and functional.

8

A Home of One's Own

Early man was a wandering hunter and food gatherer. His personal possessions were limited to what he could carry on his back, and home was whatever temporary shelter he could find or erect. It was only when he took to agriculture and settled down to village life that the possibility of permanent home ownership arose. Most primitive farming societies recognized man's innate need for a place of his own. Land was the communal property of the tribe, but the hut was usually regarded as the private possession of its builder. Even at this early date there was a distinction between the ownership of a house and the land upon which it stood. A theme had been established which was to reappear time and again in the long history of housing.

When the Sumerian civilization grew up beside the Tigris and Euphrates, the communal ownership of its land was entrusted to the priests as the representatives of the gods from whom all territorial rights were thought to stem. Not only the land but even the people who lived on it were considered the property of the gods and therefore of the temple. During the third millennium B.C., however, temporal power began to pass to successful war-chiefs, who were able to force or persuade the priests to grant them recognition as regents of the gods. The idea of kingship was born, and each local monarch claimed absolute ownership of the land, which through the stewardship of the temples had previously belonged to the whole community. Now it was possible for the king to make territorial grants to friends and servants. From 2000 B.C. onwards much of the land of Mesopotamia began to pass into private ownership. Most Sumerians still remained peasants paying a rent of farm produce to lord or temple, but a property-owning middle class was beginning to emerge.

The existence of this privileged group is confirmed by the large number of clay tablets dealing with house sales which have survived from second-millennium Mesopotamia. Such documents were written in a very business-like style. Seller and purchaser were named; the location of the house was

The stone on which Hammurabi's laws were engraved.

fixed by reference to the neighbours; the price was quoted; the sale was witnessed and dated. Transfer was clear and indisputable, but to prevent all chance of future litigation the former owner was required to take an oath renouncing all claim on the property.

Law codes dating back to the same period show that the property owner was granted a considerable degree of legal protection. Amongst the fragmentary remains of the code of Lipit-Ishtar, King of Isin from 1934 to 1924 B.C., was a law which enabled a householder to claim compensation from a neighbour if a burglar had entered his premises by way of that neighbour's uncultivated plot. The laws of the city of Eshnunna even recognized the sentimental value of a property. They provided that if a man were forced to sell his house for debt then he should have first chance to buy it when it came back on to the market. The most complete of all these early collections of laws, the famous code of Hammurabi, King of Babylon 1792 to 1750 B.C., granted every home owner the right to sell his property to whomsoever he wished or to pledge it against the payment of a debt. Householders were even safeguarded from jerrybuilding for Hammurabi decreed the death penalty for the builder of a house which collapsed and killed its owner.

In Egypt, the other ancient civilization of the Middle East, the Pharaohs of the Middle Kingdom (about 2150 to about 1800 B.C.) made grants of land to the peasants who thus became freemen with a stake in the country. Land was therefore available for ordinary men to buy and sell and build upon, but there is evidence that although the city artisan might own the fabric of his house he in some cases had to pay a rent for the ground it occupied. It must surely have been a transfer of ground rents which the sixth-century B.C. Pharaoh Apries intended when he made a gift of the entire river frontage of Memphis to the temple of Ptah. Memphis was a prosperous city and it seems inconceivable that even the king could have owned every building in its most favoured district.

During the fourth century B.C. Egypt was conquered by Alexander the Great, one of whose generals, Ptolemy, later seized the province for himself and established a dynasty, which was to endure for three centuries. Many legal papyri concerning real estate have survived from this period of Greek domination, enabling a picture to be built up of the pattern of house ownership in Ptolemaic Egypt. From the large number of contracts dealing with house leases it is clear that many people rented, rather than owned, their homes. The lessee was bound to pay an agreed rent, to look after the property, and return it in good condition to its owner when the lease expired. In return he enjoyed full rights to the house and was protected from any intrusions of the landlord. One peculiarity which the papyri bring to light is the possibility of parts of the same building belonging to different people. Partial ownership of this sort must have encouraged the letting of flats.

In Greece itself many people lived in rented accommodation. The greatest holders of property in the cities were the temples, which over the years had waxed rich on the gifts and bequests of wealthy adherents. Municipalities also often owned houses and shops, which were let out to tenants, but private landlords were by no means unknown. An account of the fourth-century B.C. lawsuit over property left by the Athenian Ciron, mentions that he owned two houses, one for letting and one for his own use. House owners could evidently do well out of renting. Not only was Ciron's estate hotly contested but the value of property was so widely recognized that the philosopher Socrates (about 469 to 399 B.C.) could make it the basis of a joke. An expert in the apparently innocent question, he once asked an acquaintance's mistress whether the money for her fine clothes came from the rent of a house.

The Roman Empire, which engulfed the Greek world in the second century B.C. and eventually grew to surround the entire Mediterranean, was tolerant of local custom where it did not impinge on the imperial power. Roman law did not recognize the separate ownership of different parts of a building, but the Egyptians were allowed to continue this custom even when their country, long a client state, was made a province of the empire in 30 B.C. Several interesting documents from Roman Egypt show that the practice of borrowing money to buy a house was well established and that on occasions the state itself was willing to act as creditor. In A.D. 130, for example, a certain Diogenes bought a house which had been confiscated by the government when its owner failed to honour a debt. The price demanded was 600 drachmas with an additional charge of one-sixteenth, probably to cover administrative costs. Diogenes lacked the ready cash but, a little surprisingly, found the state willing to advance all the money needed at an interest rate of eight per cent.

In Rome itself land was far too expensive for an ordinary person to own a house, instead most families rented a few rooms in a block of flats. The city abounded in these blocks, or 'insulae' as they were called, but Rome was such a magnet for visitors that accommodation was always scarce and, therefore, expensive. Another factor drove rents still higher. Most insula owners preferred to let their property on a five-year lease to a single principal tenant, who secured the right to rent out the premises on his own account. The unfortunate sub-tenants had to pay an exorbitant rent to provide a profit for two landlords rather than one, and many were driven to take in lodgers to help pay their quarterly dues.

Title to land or property is only of value in an orderly society. During the chaotic period which followed the collapse of Roman power in Europe, might was the only guaranty of ownership. In Britain the original inhabitants were driven into the remoter parts of the country by an influx of Germanic tribesmen. By the sixth century Roman Britain had been transformed into Saxon England.

Initially the bulk of the Anglo-Saxon population were freemen or churls who lived and worked on their own small holdings. This independence was, however, gradually eroded, and as early as A.D. 700 some peasants were reduced to renting land from a lord. Three hundred years later the descendants of such people had sunk to such a servile position that they could not leave the lord's estate without permission. At the time of the Norman Conquest very few churls in the south of England owned the land on which their homes were built.

The Anglo-Saxons were essentially a farming nation, and when King Alfred (849–901) instituted his burghal system of fortified towns to combat Viking incursions it is probable that he was forced to offer favourable tenures to lure people in from the country. Most townsmen held their tenements directly from the king to whom they owned specified duties and paid a fixed annual money rent. Already there was a difference between the countryman who paid for home and land entirely with his agricultural services or produce, and the burgess who paid mainly in cash.

Although the king always remained the principal landlord within the Anglo-Saxon boroughs, other land owners began to gain footholds as the towns prospered. To some extent this can be explained by the natural desire of a nobleman to maintain a residence in his local market town, but some magnates owned far more property than they could have needed for personal use. During the tenth century, for instance, the Abbess of Barking had twenty-eight houses in London, while Aelfgar, who held a manor in Bishopsworth, owned ten houses in Bristol. The inescapable conclusion is that it had become profitable to invest in city property. Perhaps the majority of city dwellers still owned the actual structure of their houses and merely paid a ground rent to the king, but some at least now rented accommodation from private landlords.

With the Norman Conquest a thorough going feudalism was imposed on England. Theoretically all land belonged to the king who made grants to his aristocracy in return for their military services. The tenants-in-chief divided their holdings amongst vassals of their own. This sub-division might be repeated several times. At the bottom of the feudal pyramid came the landless serfs, bound to the soil of the estate they cultivated.

Ordinary townsmen were far more fortunate than their country cousins. The fact that they paid a money ground rent for their tenements rather than a tribute of their labour left them free at a time when most men were little better than slaves. Burgage tenure under which land was held within borough boundaries often allowed the tenant to sell his buildings to whomsoever he wished without any reference to the ultimate lord of the soil. All the new owner was required to do, to ensure his possession, was continue with the customary annual rent.

However, it must not be imagined that the towns were oases of equality in the desert of feudalism. There were glaring differences between the 'haves' and the 'have-nots', which widened as time went on. In great cities all over Europe—London, Paris, Cologne—merchants advanced in wealth and power while the artisans grew relatively poorer. By the twelfth century the great mass of townsmen lived in property they did not own. As the fourteenth-century English poet William Langland remarked bitterly in his 'Piers Plowman': 'They (the merchants) buy houses, they become landlords, if they sold honestly they would not build so high.'

The decay of feudalism during the latter half of the fourteenth century gave many agricultural serfs an opportunity to escape from bondage. By the early fifteen century the tribute of labour was increasingly being commuted to a money payment. Villeins became free yeomen renting rather than bound to the fields of their lords. Few, however, could aspire to the actual ownership of land and home. The change from a feudal to a money economy gave the countryman his freedom but left most of the land in the possession of the old aristocracy. In the towns the merchants also retained their grip and most property remained in their hands. It was to be centuries before any but the most thrifty of workers could hope to scrape enough capital together to buy a house of his own.

Feudalism had, with all its faults, imposed duties on the lord as well as demanding service from the vassal. On its breakdown the profit motive began to predominate over the older feelings of mutual responsibility. Landlords became less concerned with what was fair than with what they thought could be exacted from their tenants. By the sixteenth century house rent swallowed up a large proportion of the urban workman's income. In London where accommodation was always scarce and rents particularly high, even the peers of the realm were prepared to seek a profit. John Stow in his sixteenth-century *Survey of London* described, for instance, the fate of an old mansion called 'Cold Harbrough' belonging to the Earl of Shrewsbury, who 'took it down, and in place thereof built a great number of small tenements, now letten out for great rents to people of all sorts'.

The almost intolerable burden which rents placed on the poorer inhabitants of London is shown by the exodus which followed the Great Fire of 1666. Even before the flames engulfed 13,000 of the capital's half-timbered houses accommodation had been extremely expensive. Samuel Pepys, the diarist, recorded a conversation with a friend who claimed to have 'computed that the rents of the houses lost this fire in the City comes to £600,000 per annum'. The cost of re-building in brick drove prices still higher and many Londoners were forced to migrate to other towns or to move into the surrounding country districts.

Conditions were no better during the next century when Jonathan Swift, author of *Gulliver's Travels*, could complain of the 'plaguey deep' rent of eight shillings a week which he was forced to pay for two rooms in central London. Even the wealthy often rented accommodation, and a fashionable gentleman might have to pay £200 a year or more for a house in a favoured square. Compared with such London prices the rentals of agricultural cottages were extremely moderate, but at a time when a labourer in southern England was lucky to receive six shillings a week they could hardly be anything else.

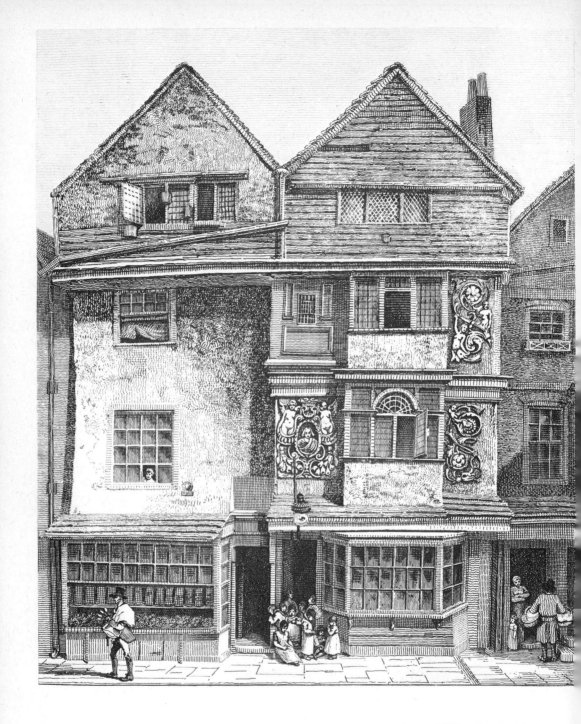

A merchant's house in Stuart London. As early as the fourteenth century the poet William Langland had complained that if merchants sold honestly 'they would not build so high'. However, these tall houses did provide shelter for numerous domestics and apprentices, as well as the master's own family.

This was a period when a steady increase in Britain's population and a slow drift from country into town put a mounting strain on urban housing resources. With the onset of industrialization in the last decades of the eighteenth century the tempo of change quickened. What had been a trickle of people leaving the farms had, by the early 1800s, become a flood. Old centres of population were swamped; villages mushroomed into full-blown towns. Factory owners and speculative builders threw up thousands of new houses, but demand always seemed to exceed supply. Rents were so high and wages so low that many of the new industrial workers were forced to live in dreadfully overcrowded conditions. Only the fortunate enjoyed a room to themselves, and many had no other lodging than a rented share in another person's bed. There was little to encourage the working man other than his sturdy belief in self-help.

Even before the Industrial Revolution created a host of new problems it had become common in certain parts of Britain for neighbours to club together for mutual protection in what were called 'friendly societies'. Members paid a regular contribution into their society's funds and in return were guaranteed assistance if they fell on hard times. Daniel Defoe noted and praised the friendly societies which were active in the Bristol area as early as the 1690s. A hundred years later such clubs had become a familiar feature in the communal life of the developing industrial centres. The more intelligent artisans realized that their only chance for some kind of security lay in combining their own efforts at saving with those of others of a like mind. It was probably this firmly established tradition of working-class self-help which gave a group of Birmingham artisans the confidence to embark on what must have seemed a daring new venture in co-operation — the formation of a building society.

The idea of combining to build homes seems to have been born over a pint of ale. The friends and neighbours who met regularly during the 1770s in the Golden Cross Inn on Birmingham's Snow Hill must often have complained of high rents, and regretted that none had the money to buy a house of his own. Then someone had an inspiration. Why not form a society, save up, pool their resources, and purchase some land. Then as more subscriptions came in houses could be built and let to members selected by lot. Rents would be levied and paid into the funds to help build more houses until every subscriber had a home of his own and the society could be wound up. Richard Ketley, the innkeeper, scenting profit in a club based on his premises, encouraged the project, and what was probably the world's first building society was formed at the Golden Cross in or around 1775.

News of the enterprise spread and similar societies began to spring up

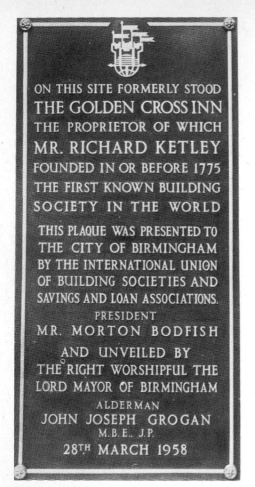

ON THIS SITE FORMERLY STOOD
THE GOLDEN CROSS INN
THE PROPRIETOR OF WHICH
MR. RICHARD KETLEY
FOUNDED IN OR BEFORE 1775
THE FIRST KNOWN BUILDING
SOCIETY IN THE WORLD

THIS PLAQUE WAS PRESENTED TO
THE CITY OF BIRMINGHAM
BY THE INTERNATIONAL UNION
OF BUILDING SOCIETIES AND
SAVINGS AND LOAN ASSOCIATIONS.
PRESIDENT
MR. MORTON BODFISH
AND UNVEILED BY
THE RIGHT WORSHIPFUL THE
LORD MAYOR OF BIRMINGHAM
ALDERMAN
JOHN JOSEPH GROGAN
M.B.E., J.P.
28TH MARCH 1958

Memorial plaque on the site of the Golden Cross, *Birmingham, where the world's first building society was founded in about 1775.*

throughout the Midlands and the industrial North. By the end of the century at least fifty had been founded, but with the disappearance of their records little is known of most of them other than their names. The building club established in the village of Longridge near Preston in 1793 is, however, an exception. Not only has its account book survived, but the row of houses which its members built between 1795 and 1799 is still standing as a witness of the society's success. These homes are the earliest which have been positively identified as the work of a building society.

The building clubs of the eighteenth century were very different from their modern descendants. They were small local concerns, few having many more than twenty members, and their sole aim was to actually build new homes for their subscribers. In the early days existing houses were never purchased. Once the purpose of a society had been achieved and all its houses were built and paid for, it was automatically terminated.

174

Such small, transitory clubs could help only a few on the road to home ownership, and although Britain waxed rich during the nineteenth century on the proceeds of its industry it remained predominantly a nation of renters. The Englishman might boast that his home was his castle, but it was a castle which belonged to someone else. The building societies were eventually to revolutionize the pattern of home ownership; first, however, they had to change and develop themselves.

By the 1840s termination was proving a hindrance to the further expansion of the movement. Once a society had begun it was practically impossible to attract new members because few could afford the 'back payments' required to bring them in step with those who had joined at the start. Some societies partially overcame the difficulty by initiating fresh issues of shares— effectively new terminating societies—whenever demand accumulated, but in those days of primitive accounting it proved all too easy to get the funds of the various issues inextricably mixed. It was at this point that a young accountant, Arthur Scratchley, appeared on the scene and with clear, incisive logic cleared the way for further progress. The essence of his plan was to make the building society permanent, with the members who dropped out once their house was purchased being replaced by newcomers. Since

Club Row, Longridge, built between 1795 and 1799. The earliest houses identified as the work of a building society.

the society had no fixed termination date new members would be able to join at any time without the need to make crippling back payments. Scratchley also differentiated between two classes of member—the borrowers and the investors. Investors were to be paid $4\frac{1}{2}$ or 5 per cent compound interest on their subscriptions, while borrowers drawing money to build or buy houses were to pay $6\frac{1}{2}$ or 7 per cent on their debt. Funds accruing from this difference in interest rates would be used to meet the society's expenses. The foundations of the modern building society had been well and truly laid.

Permanent societies appeared in 1846, but it was many years before the idea really caught on. As late as 1875, the hundredth anniversary of the movement, old-style terminating societies still remained dominant in Lancashire, South Wales, and the northeast of England, despite the growth of large permanent organizations in London and the towns of Yorkshire. It has been estimated that by its centenary year the movement could boast a total membership of investors and borrowers approaching 400,000. This was, however, spread over some 2,500 societies, so that the majority must have continued small and local. The bulk of the population were still too poor to benefit from the services which the building societies had to offer.

To many reformers it appeared impossible for any but a small minority of the country's workers to aspire to home ownership. What was needed, it seemed, was Parliamentary legislation to sweep away the appalling industrial slums and promote the building of decent rented accommodation. Governmental intervention in the form of a succession of well-meaning Acts proved, however, largely ineffectual. The Shaftesbury Acts of 1851 gave Local Authorities the power to build and inspect lodging houses; the Torrens Act of 1868 conferred the right to demolish insanitary houses; the Cross Act of 1875 allowed the clearance of large areas of slum property. If these Acts had been firmly applied the working classes could have looked forward to a rapid improvement in their living conditions. Unfortunately, the legislation was permissive and left Local Authorities completely free to decide whether or not to use their powers. The good intentions of the reformers ran up against a stone wall of municipal indifference and sloth. It was not until the housing Act of 1890 that a clear responsibility was laid on Local Authorities to demolish slums and replace them with something better. The way was now opened for the development of council housing.

The twentieth century began with an already strong building society movement and a new-found municipal commitment to better housing. Eventually these two forces were to alter the whole pattern of home owner-ship in Britain, but in the years immediately prior to the First World War

Houses built in the inter-war years for the owner-occupier.

their influence seemed negligible. Nine out of ten houses were still rented from private landlords. During the inter-war years the picture began to change. Returning soldiers had been promised 'homes for heroes', and with a flurry of building subsidies, rent controls, and council-estate construction the Government endeavoured to keep its word. Between 1918 and 1939 well over a million houses were built for Local Authorities, while private enterprise provided another two million, nine hundred thousand. Most of the latter were bought by would-be owner-occupiers with the help of building society loans. Quietly and without fuss a social revolution was taking place.

By shortly after the Second World War the number of privately-rented houses had dropped to about half the national total while those in the hands of owner-occupiers had risen to close on a third. Since then the importance of the private landlord has continued to decline and council housing now accounts for nearly 70 per cent of all rented accommodation. More dramatic, however, has been the continuing success of the building societies in promoting home ownership. Today, on the eve of the movement's two-hundredth anniversary, half of Britain's houses are owner-occupied. The men of the Golden Cross who started it all would be well pleased with their memorial.

177

This discussion of house ownership in the modern world has naturally been centred on British experience but we can at least glance at the way in which the people of other countries have attempted to satisfy the age-old human need for a home. Continental Europeans have, in general, been less concerned with ownership than the British. Fifty per cent of the dwellings in such great cities as Copenhagen, Hamburg, Paris, and Stockholm are still rented from private landlords, while in Amsterdam the figure is as high as three in every four. Building societies have taken root in Germany,

A housing society scheme in central London consisting of 300 flats. Although the dwellings always remain the property of the society, once the cost of the home has been paid, rents are reduced to cover maintenance only.

Scandinavia, and Holland, but they have not found the soil as fertile as they did in Britain.

The United States, on the other hand, has a tradition of private ownership which goes back to the War of Independence. Thomas Jefferson, one of the founders of the Republic, was adamant that '. . . as few as possible shall be without a little portion of land . . .'. In such a climate building societies were bound to thrive. The first in America was founded in 1831 at Frankford near Philadelphia by three settlers who had carried the idea with them from England. Other societies quickly sprang up in places as far apart as New York and South Carolina. By the 1880s there was scarcely a state in the Union which was without what was by then called a 'Building and Loan Association'. These associations have played a major part in the unprecedented advance in home ownership which has occurred in modern America where two families in three live in a house which they themselves own.

Today house ownership is more widespread than it has been for centuries. Even the Soviet citizens can opt to buy his co-operative flat rather than continue to pay a rent. All, however, is far from right with the world's housing. Conditions in the developed countries make it impossible for the individual to build himself a shelter and since he cannot help himself the state must assume a measure of responsibility. No society which fails to provide decent accommodation for its members can consider itself successful. A place to live should be everyone's birthright; a place which they own remains most people's dream.

Suggestions for Further Reading

1   The Development of the House

Braun, H., *Old English Houses* (London: Faber and Faber, 1962)
Carcopino, J., *Daily Life in Ancient Rome* (London: Penguin Books, 1962)
Lloyd, N., *A History of the English House* (London: The Architectural Press, 1931, reprint 1949)
Saggs, H. W. F., *The Greatness that was Babylon* (London: Sidgwick and Jackson, 1962)
Wycherley, R. E., *How the Greeks Built Cities* (London: Macmillan, second edition 1967)

2   Home Cooking

Chandler, D. and Lacey, A. D., *The Rise of the Gas Industry in Britain* (London: British Gas Council, 1949)
Clair, C., *Kitchen and Table* (London: Abelard-Schuman, 1964)
Giedion, S., *Mechanization Takes Command* (New York: Oxford University Press, 1949)
Harrison, M., *The Kitchen in History* (Reading: Osprey, 1972)

3   Heating the Home

Fletcher, V., *Chimney Pots and Stacks* (Arundel: Centaur Press, 1968)
Peirce, J., *Fire on the Hearth* (Springfield, Mass.: Pond-Ekberg, 1951)
Wood, M., *The English Mediaeval House* (London: Phoenix House, 1965)
Wright, L., *Home Fires Burning* (London: Routledge & Kegan Paul, 1964)

4   A Light in the Window

Chandler, D. and Lacey, A. D., *The Rise of the Gas Industry in Britain* (London: British Gas Council, 1949)

O'Dea, W. T., *The Social History of Lighting* (London: Routledge & Kegan Paul, 1958)

Thwing, L., *Flickering Flames* (London: Bell, 1959)

Wood, M., *The English Mediaeval House* (London: Phoenix House, 1965)

5 Water

Furon, R., *The Problem of Water* (London: Faber and Faber, 1967)

Hartley, D., *Water in England* (London: Macdonald, 1964)

Metropolitan Water Board, *The Water Supply of London* (London: M.W.B., 1961)

Robins, F. W., *The Story of Water Supply* (London: Oxford University Press, 1946)

Wright, L., *Clean and Decent* (London: Routledge & Kegan Paul, 1960)

6 A Place Without

Palmer, R., *The Water Closet* (Newton Abbot: David & Charles, 1973)

Wright, L., *Clean and Decent* (London: Routledge & Kegan Paul, 1960)

7 Making a House a Home

Burton, E., *The Elizabethans at Home* (London: Longman, 1958)

Entwisle, E. A., *The Book of Wallpaper* (London: Arthur Barker, 1954)

Hayward, H. (Editor), *World Furniture* (London: Paul Hamlyn, 1965)

Mercer, E., *Furniture 700–1700* (London: Weidenfeld and Nicolson, 1969)

Savage, G., *A Concise History of Interior Decoration* (London: Thames and Hudson, 1966)

Yarwood, D., *The English Home* (London: Batsford, 1956)

8 A Home of One's Own

Price, S. J., *Building Societies* (London: Franey & Co., Ltd., 1956)

Acknowledgements

Acknowledgements are due to the following for permission to reproduce pictures on the pages indicated: Academie des Sciences de Bulgarie, Institut Archeologique, Sofia, 143; Bernan, W., *On the History and Art of Warming and Ventilating Rooms and Buildings* (Bell, 1845), 67B, 70; The British Library Board, 39, 93; The Trustees of the British Museum, 12, 35, 36, 41, 45, 89, 90, 105, 111, 116, 145, 146, 147, 150, 160; *The Builder* (Vol. 7, 1849), 136, (21 April, 1849) 139, (3 July, 1852) 137T, (17 July, 1852) 137B, (Vol. 10, 1852) 138, (5 November, 1853) 29, (30 July, 1853) 120; Cantacuzino, M., *European Domestic Architecture* (Studio Vista, 1970), 13T, 13B; Clark, G. and Piggott, S., *Prehistoric Societies* (Hutchinson, 1965), 8, 11; Photo Deutsches Museum, München, 33; Edwards, F., *On the Extravagant Use of Fuel in Cooking Operations* (1869), 47, 50T; Trustees of Sir Arthur Evans' Estate, 103; Von Falke, J., *Art in the House* (1879), 156, 157; Fishenden, *House Heating* (Witherby, 1925), 67T, 74; Reproduced by permission of the Syndics of the Fitzwilliam Museum, Cambridge, 37, 106; Garrett, R. & A., *Suggestions for House Decoration* (Macmillan, 1876), 163; Germanisches Nationalmuseum, Nürnberg, 68; From a print by James Gillray (1787), 46; Greater London Council Photograph Library, 30; Havard, *Dictionnaire de l'Ameublement* (Paris, 1890–94), 126; Hellyer, S. S., *The Plumber and Sanitary Houses* (1877), 134, *Principles and Practice of Plumbing* (1891), 133; The Housing Corporation, 178; Hygena Limited, 54; Kansas State Historical Society, Topeka, 69; Louvre Museum, Paris, 167; Mansell-Alinari, 18; Morse, E. S., *Japanese Homes and Their Surroundings* (Sampson Low, 1888), 87; Nash, J., *The Mansions of England in the Olden Time* (Third Series) (1839, 1845), 59, 158; The National Gallery of Scotland, 112; National Tourist Organization of Greece, London, 14; Nelson Gallery—Atkins Museum, Kansas City, Missouri (Nelson Fund), 15; The Oriental Institute, The University of Chicago, 80; Parker, J. H., *Domestic Architecture in England from Richard II to Henry VIII* (1853, 1859), 63, 83, 84T, 84B, 109, 110, 128; Payne, *Royal Dresden Gallery* (c. 1845), 115, 152;

Phillips, R. R., *The Sevantless House* (1920), 121; *The Pictorial Gallery of Arts* (*c.* 1846), 25, 38, 57, 58, 91, 117; Prado Museum, Madrid, 62; Price, Seymour J., *Building Societies: Their Origin and History* (Franey, 1958), 174, 175; Courtesy of Anthony Ridley, 23, 24, 26, 56, 64, 65, 86, 124, 132, 172, 177; From a sketch by Rowlandson, 162; Photo Science Museum, London, 49, 51, 88, 94, 96, 99, 130; Crown Copyright, Science Museum, London, 50B, 53, 73, 76, 97; From 'A Neolithic City in Turkey' by James Mellaert Copyright © (April 1964) by Scientific American, Inc. All rights reserved, 9; The Scottish Tourist Board, 27, 144; Solar Heat Limited, Kings Norton, Birmingham, 77; Staatliche Antikensammlungen und Glyptothek, München, 148; Thomas, *The Ventilation, Heating and Lighting of Dwellings* (Longmans, 1906), 75; Photo Jerry Tubby, 164; Turner, T. H., *Some Account of Domestic Architecture in England from the Conquest to the End of the Thirteenth Century* (1877), 20, 21, 22, 40, 61T, 61B, 81; Twyfords Limited, 119, 140; Viollet-le-Duc, *Dictionnaire Raisonné du Mobilier Français* (1858), 153, 154, 155; Courtesy of Sir Mortimer Wheeler, 102; Wilkinson, *A Popular Account of the Ancient Egyptians* (1854), 33; Wright, T., *The Homes of Other Days*, 42, 43.

Index

Figures in bold type denote pictures